GIANTS
OF
OCTOBER

2014 WORLD SERIES CHAMPIONS

Katherine Grigsby, Layout & Design

ISBN: 978-1-940056-13-5

Printed in the United States of America
KCI Sports Publishing   3340 Whiting Avenue, Suite 5   Stevens Point, WI 54481
Phone: 1-800-697-3756   Fax: 715-344-2668
www.kcisports.com

WORLD SERIES CHAMPIONS

The San Francisco Giants celebrate after Game 7 of baseball's World Series against the Kansas City Royals. The Giants won 3-2 to win the series.
AP Photo/Matt Slocum

GIANTS LOOK TO REBOUND IN 2014

With World Series championships in both 2010 and 2012 San Francisco fans like to point to a calendar and recent history as indication that 2014 - another even numbered calendar year – will provide the Giants will all of the good karma they will need to bring home yet another championship.

And although there are positive vibes emanating out of Arizona, the reality is that in 2013 these Giants went from the pinnacle of the baseball world to being an afterthought in the NL West finishing with a disappointing 76-86 record.

At the conclusion of last season Giants GM Brian Sabean, the longest tenured GM in the game, knew wholesale changes in the offseason were not the answer. He has been around long enough to know that making a few key acquisitions – and getting and staying healthy - will

Facing Page: Giants Bruce Bochy during a Spring Training game against the Brewers at Scottsdale Stadium in Scottsdale, AZ. The Giants beat the Brewers 4-3.
AP Photo/Micah Tapman

Above: San Franciscos' third base coach Tim Flannery congratulates Hunter Pence on his solo home run off Royals relief pitcher Wade Davis in Surprise, Ariz.
AP Photo/Tony Gutierrez

The San Francisco Giants run before a spring training workout in Arizona.
AP Photo/Darron Cummings

likely be enough for the Giants to be in contention in 2014.

Sabean and his staff went to work and pulled off a major coup in free-agency when veteran pitcher Tim Hudson agreed to sign with the Giants. Hudson provides an immediate upgrade to the starting rotation. If Matt Cain and Tim Lincecum can return to anything close to their 2012 levels, and if Madison Bumgarner is Madison Baumgarner, the Giants will roll out one of the top rotations in the game. Jeremy Affeldt, Javier Lopez, Sergio Romo and Santiago Casilla form the backbone of an effective relief corps.

Sabean also signed free-agent Michael Morse who will be penciled in to open the season as the starting left fielder. If he can stay healthy, Morse's presence will add a powerful bat to the Giants lineup.

As is his hallmark, the Giants GM chose familiarity over the unknown when he resigned several Giants players whose contracts were up after the 2013 campaign. Lincecum, Hunter Pence, Javier Lopez and Ryan Vogelsong all remain with the Orange and Black.

Buster Posey (28) hangs on to a foul ball hit by Brewers' Wily Peralta as Brandon Hicks (14) backs Posey up during the third inning of a spring training baseball game in Phoenix. The Giants defeated the Brewers 5-4.
AP Photo/Ross D. Franklin

Along with homegrown talents Buster Posey, Baumgarner, Pablo Sandoval, Brandon Belt, and Brandon Crawford the experience that has been the hallmark of past championship teams is in place heading into 2014.

On paper the Giants are an intriguing team with the pieces in place to make a run at another World Series. The NL West looks like it'll be competitive throughout, and with Los Angeles wedging a few more high-priced additions into their roster the Dodgers will have a say in who wins the division title.

But with a future Hall-of-Fame manager, a starting rotation potentially as good as any in the National League and a group of seasoned veterans with big game experience something tells us these Giants will be a tough out come October.

A large flag is presented in the AT&T Park outfield during the national anthem before the opening day baseball game in San Francisco.
AP Photo/Jeff Chiu

APRIL 8, 2014 AT&T PARK

GIANTS 7 • DIAMONDBACKS 3

GIANTS WIN HOME OPENER

THERE IS NOTHING LIKE OPENING DAY

SAN FRANCISCO, CALIFORNIA

The San Francisco Giants continued their hot start to 2014 and this time they had 42,000 loyal fans cheering them on.

Newly acquired Michael Morse hit a two-run single and Brandon Belt hit a two-run homer for San Francisco in a 7-3 win against the Arizona Diamondbacks.

Starting pitcher Tim Hudson – acquired in November on a two-year, $23 million dollar deal - followed up 7 2/3 scoreless innings at Arizona last Wednesday with another strong outing. He allowed three runs -- two earned -- and seven hits with four strikeouts and no walks in a 101-pitch performance.

"It's hard to pitch better than he did the first two starts," manager Bruce Bochy said.

"Definitely I'll take these first two starts," Hudson said.

Miles Scott, left, dressed as Batkid, poses for photographs with San Francisco Giants pitcher Matt Cain after throwing the ceremonial first pitch. Scott, a Northern California boy with leukemia, fought villains and rescued a damsel in distress as a caped crusader through The Greater Bay Area Make-A-Wish Foundation.
AP Photo/Eric Risberg, Pool

Above: Giants pitcher Tim Hudson delivers a pitch against Arizona on Opening Day.
AP Photo/Jeff Chiu

Facing Page: Michael Morse drills a fifth-inning double on Opening Day.
AP Photo/Eric Risberg

"It's been a long road for me to get here," Hudson said. "I'm just thrilled to be back out there pitching and competing, feeling somewhat healthy. I couldn't ask for a better start to the year."

Belt's drive off Trevor Cahill (0-3) gave him five homers and the Giants a majors-leading 12.

New Giants left fielder Morse emphatically pumped his fist at first base after a third-inning single, then added a two-out double in the fifth. San Francisco scored four runs with two outs.

MAY 25, 2014 AT&T PARK

GIANTS 8 • TWINS 1

A TWINS SWEEPING

SAN FRANCISCO, CALIFORNIA

Madison Bumgarner pitched seven strong innings, the San Francisco hitters jumped all over Minnesota Twins starter Ricky Nolasco and the Giants completed a three-game sweep of the Twins with an 8-1 win Sunday.

The Giants jumped on Nolasco early with a pair of bloop singles in the first and a run-scoring hit by Pablo Sandoval that left fielder Eduardo Nunez got a late jump on. Michael Morse's sacrifice fly made it 2-0.

Tucker Pence's home run in the bottom of the third gave the Giants a 3-1 lead.

Morse doubled and scored in the fourth and then went back to work in the fifth inning drilling a bases-loaded double – one of three Morse doubles on the day. As he stood on second base he pumped his fist prompting a loud ovation from the AT&T Park crowd.

"Moments like that make you feel so humble and happy that you're here," said Morse, who signed a one-year deal with San Francisco in the offseason. "Every day feels like the playoffs here. It's awesome."

Bumgarner (6-3) earned his fourth straight win while relying mainly on his fastball and slider to baffle the slumping Twins. He struck out 10 with no walks and allowed only two runners past second base.

"Madison was Madison," Giants manager Bruce Bochy said. "He had his normal stuff and pitched great."

It was a far different result than

Giants' Michael Morse hits a three-run double off Twins pitcher Ricky Nolasco during the fifth inning.
AP Photo/Jeff Chiu

San Francisco pitcher Madison Bumgarner throws against the Minnesota Twins on Sunday, May 25, 2014.
AP Photo/Jeff Chiu

Minnesota Twins' Danny Santana (39) slides into second base as shortstop Brandon Crawford applies the tag.
AP Photo/Jeff Chiu

Bumgarner got in his only other appearance against Minnesota in 2011 when the left-hander was knocked out of the game after retiring one batter.

"I for sure didn't forget about that," said Bumgarner, who reached double digits in strikeouts for the 15th time in his career. "There wasn't a whole lot of talk about it but it's something that's tough to forget, to go through a start like that one."

George Kontos pitched the final two innings for San Francisco, which has won seven straight games against American League teams dating to 2013.

JUNE 8, 2014 AT&T PARK

GIANTS 6 • METS 4

GIANTS ROLL TO 5th STRAIGHT

SAN FRANCISCO, CALIFORNIA

After knocking off the New York Mets 6-4 on Sunday for their fourth sweep of the season, the Giants have now won 14 of their last 17 games and own baseball's best record at 42-21. They also own a 9 ½ game lead over the Los Angeles Dodgers in the NL West.

Does it get any better than this?

"There's nothing I can complain about," manager Bruce Bochy said.

"We're going to ride it out, ride the wave," said Tim Lincecum, who allowed six hits, struck out six and walked one in six innings of work. "It's fun to be a part of."

Gregor Blanco provided the offensive firepower with a double, single and three runs driven in. His two-run double capped a three-run second for the Giants and they never looked back.

"We do have confidence," Blanco said. "Anytime we see ourselves losing a game, for some reason, we step it up. For some reason, we get mad and things start happening."

"The club is getting contributions from everybody," Bochy said. "Last year, it seemed like your hope is through the heart of the order and then you have to wait for them to come back around."

Four relievers held the Mets to one run in two innings before Sergio Romo recorded his 20th save of the season.

Giants' Sergio Romo celebrates after the final out is made against the New York Mets. The Giants won, 6-4.
AP Photo/Ben Margot

Giants' Gregor Blanco swings for a two run double off New York Mets' Zack Wheeler in the second inning on Sunday, June 8, 2014.
AP Photo/Ben Margot

Brandon Crawford watches his three-run double as the Giants beat the Phillies 9-6 in 14 innings.
AP Photo/Michael Perez

JULY 22, 2014 CITIZENS BANK PARK

GIANTS 9 • PHILLIES 6

CRAWFORD'S DOUBLE LIFTS GIANTS IN 14

PHILADELPHIA, PENNSYLVANIA

It took 14-innings and nine San Francisco Giants pitchers but Bruce Bochy got his win.

Brandon Crawford drilled a bases-clearing double in the top of the 14th inning to provide the difference in the Giants marathon 9-6 win over Philadelphia Tuesday night.

Giants manager Bruce Bochy was running out of available arms. The idea of using a position player to throw an inning was being considered. Thanks to Crawford, Bochy didn't have to make the unusual move.

"It was huge," Bochy said of the hit. "George [Kontos] might have one more inning at that point."

Kontos didn't have one more inning. The reliever got just one out before Tim Lincecum, San Francisco's ninth pitcher, came on to record the final two outs for the save. Had the game still been tied, Bochy

Pablo Sandoval, left, and Buster Posey, right, watch Gregor Blanco score on a Brandon Crawford double that scored three runs in the fourteenth inning.
AP Photo/Michael Perez

Pablo Sandoval works on his bubble gum blowing skills between pitches.
AP Photo/Michael Perez

Sandoval made a great effort on a pop foul hit by the Phillies' Ben Revere in the first inning.
AP Photo/Michael Perez

was considering outfielder Tyler Colvin.

"I asked him if he had pitched before, and he mentioned high school," Bochy said.

Crawford snapped a 2-for-22 skid with his two-out hit off the wall in left-center field and finished with four RBIs. Buster Posey, who doubled and scored in the 14th, sent the game into extras with a solo homer in the ninth off Jonathan Papelbon, who blew his third save. Kontos (3-0) allowed one run in 2 1/3 innings to earn the win for the second straight night.

"That's why you keep your arm in good shape," Kontos said. "We'll see how I feel tomorrow – try to give them an inning or two."

The Giants (56-44) improved to 8-2 in extra-inning games and 6-0 on the road.

Posey had four hits, including two doubles, two runs and an RBI. Hunter Pence had three hits, including a fifth-inning homer.

Yusmeiro Petit, making a spot start for injured Matt Cain, allowed seven hits across five innings, struck out five and walked two.

SEPT 25, 2014 AT&T PARK

GIANTS 9 • PADRES 8

GIANTS CLINCH WILD CARD

GIANTS BACK IN THE POSTSEASON ONCE AGAIN

SAN FRANCISCO, CALIFORNIA

The Giants secured a wild card when Milwaukee lost at Cincinnati on Thursday afternoon. Then they gave up a six-run lead in their own game against San Diego before rallying for a 9-8 victory over the Padres.

Once the game was over, fireworks went off from the center-field scoreboard and Giants players gathered in the middle of the diamond to pull on playoff shirts and caps as the remaining part of the sellout crowd cheered.

"They were just so

determined to find a way to win that game so they could make this celebration that much sweeter," manager Bruce Bochy said between

Facing Page: Giants' Hunter Pence celebrates in the locker room after clinching a wildcard in the National League West in San Francisco.
AP Photo/Tony Avelar

Above: San Franciscos' Brandon Belt, left, is congratulated by teammate Brandon Crawford after hitting a solo home run against the Padres during the second inning.
AP Photo/Tony Avelar

San Francisco Giants manager Bruce Bochy, right, waves to the crowd after a 9-8 victory against the San Diego Padres.
AP Photo/Tony Avelar

swigs. "You're up six runs and you cough that up, that's disheartening, but I thought that game was indicative of our season the way they fought back and found a way to get it done."

It was a quirky way to clinch, and the Giants had no complaints.

"We got our foot in the door," Tim Hudson said. "We've obviously still got some work ahead of us these next four days. We have to win out or win three out of four and we've got a chance to be playing here. We're taking these games seriously and we have to win as many as we can."

The Giants remained one game behind Pittsburgh for the top spot in the wild-card standings, and the Pirates – 10-1 winners at Atlanta – hold the tiebreaker if the clubs finish with identical records. The Giants have the tiebreaker with St. Louis.

"You do want this to get done, because it does allow you to do some things you might not be able to do if you're not in," Bochy said. "Sure, we would have loved to come crashing in the front door instead of sliding in the back door, but this works."

The Giants won the NL West on their way to winning the World Series in each of their previous two postseason trips in 2010 and 2012. It has not been lost on Giants fans that they are back in 2014 – another even

Giants pitcher Yusmeiro Petit follows through on a delivery to the San Diego Padres during the first inning.
AP Photo/Tony Avelar

year.

And many of these players, like Buster Posey, Pablo Sandoval and Hunter Pence, have experience in pressure-packed elimination games.

"It's definitely a little bit different, because we didn't actually win to get in," shortstop Brandon Crawford said. "But we're one of the 10 teams to get in the postseason and that's the goal at the start of the year, to get in the postseason and eventually win it all. We're excited, no matter how we got in."

San Franciscos' Brandon Crawford hits a grand slam off Pittsburgh starting pitcher Edinson Volquez.
AP Photo/Gene J. Puskar

GIANTS RIDE BUMGARNER TO WILD CARD WIN

PITTSBURGH, PENNSYLVANIA

It's October and the San Francisco Giants are back to their winning ways.

Madison Bumgarner threw a complete game four-hitter and Brandon Crawford blasted a fourth-inning grand slam to lead the Giants to an 8-0 victory over the Pittsburgh Pirates in the National League wild-card game Wednesday night

It should be no surprise Bumgarner and his Giants teammates rose to the occasion.

"We thrive in these situations," Crawford said. "I don't know what it is. We just keep fighting no matter what the circumstance."

"If you don't want to pitch in these games, you probably need to find something else to do," Bumgarner said.

It was the Giants eighth consecutive postseason win and seventh straight with their season on the line, a streak that dates back to their run to a World Series title in 2012.

"We've been through it before, a lot

San Franciscos' starting pitcher Madison Bumgarner throws against the Pittsburgh Pirates the NL wild-card playoff game in Pittsburgh. *AP Photo/Don Wright*

San Francisco right fielder Hunter Pence (8) bumps into second baseman Joe Panik after Panik caught a fly ball by Pirates' Gaby Sanchez in Pittsburgh.
(AP Photo/Don Wright)

of this team has," Brandon Belt said. "We used that experience tonight. We know when we get in these situations we're going to have a good ballclub."

Particularly, when Bumgarner is on the mound. He tossed a four-hitter with 10 strikeouts, needing 109 pitches to put a quick end to Pittsburgh's second straight playoff appearance.

Mixing his fastball with a slider and curve the Pirates rarely touched, Bumgarner was in complete control and looked very much like the ace who won 18 games during San Francisco's bumpy regular season.

Overpowering one of the NL's best lineups, Bumgarner walked one and threw 79 strikes in his latest stellar October performance. The big left-hander, who allowed only four singles, has thrown 15 scoreless innings in two World Series starts.

"We got outplayed tonight," Pittsburgh second baseman Neil Walker said. "Bumgarner went out there and did what he wanted to do. He put up the strike zone and he made it tough on us."

Belt drove in three runs as the Giants padded the lead late. By then the black-clad crowd that began the night in a frenzy was watching in dismayed silence.

"We've been there before," Belt said. "It's a lot of fun when you're on the road. You know you're doing something good when the crowd goes silent."

Giants 8, Pirates 0
October 1, 2014, PNC Park, Pittsburgh, PA

	1	2	3	4	5	6	7	8	9	R	H	E
SF	0	0	0	4	0	1	2	1	0	8	11	2
PIT	0	0	0	0	0	0	0	0	0	0	4	0

GIANTS	AB	R	H	RBI	BB	SO	AVG
Blanco CF	4	1	0	0	1	0	.000
Panik 2B	5	0	3	0	0	0	.600
Posey C	5	1	2	1	0	0	.400
Sandoval 3B	4	2	2	0	1	1	.500
Arias 3B	0	0	0	0	0	0	---
Pence RF	4	2	1	0	1	0	.250
Belt 1B	3	1	2	3	2	0	.667
Crawford SS	5	1	1	4	0	2	.200
Ishikawa LF	2	0	0	0	1	1	.000
Perez PR-LF	1	0	0	0	0	0	.000
Bumgarner P	4	0	0	0	0	3	.000
Totals	37	8	11	8	6	7	

HR – B Crawford (1, 4th inning off E Volquez 3 on, 0 Out), RBI – B Crawford 4 (4), B Belt 3 (3), B Posey (1), **2-out RBI** – B Posey, LOB – 8, E – B Crawford (1, ground ball); J Arias (1, throw)

PIRATES	AB	R	H	RBI	BB	SO	AVG
Harrison 3B	4	0	2	0	0	1	.500
Mercer SS	4	0	0	0	0	2	.000
McCutchen CF	3	0	0	0	1	1	.000
Martin C	4	0	1	0	0	0	.250
Marte LF	4	0	1	0	0	1	.250
Walker 2B	4	0	0	0	0	2	.000
Sanchez 1B	3	0	0	0	0	0	.000
Snider RF	2	0	0	0	0	2	.000
Hughes P	0	0	0	0	0	0	---
LaFromboise P	0	0	0	0	0	0	---
Holdzkom P	0	0	0	0	0	0	---
Morel PH	1	0	0	0	0	0	.000
Melancon P	0	0	0	0	0	0	---
Volquez P	1	0	0	0	0	0	.000
Wilson P	0	0	0	0	0	0	---
Tabata RF	2	0	0	0	0	1	.000
Totals	32	0	4	0	1	10	

LOB – 6

GIANTS	IP	H	R	ER	BB	SO	ERA
Bumgarner (W)	9.0	4	0	0	1	10	0.00
Totals	9.0	4	0	0	1	10	

PIRATES	IP	H	R	ER	BB	SO	ERA
Volquez (L)	5.0	5	5	5	3	3	9.00
Wilson	0.1	1	0	0	1	1	0.00
Hughes	1.0	3	2	2	1	1	18.00
LaFromboise	0.2	0	0	0	0	0	0.00
Holdzkom	1.0	2	1	1	1	1	9.00
Melancon	1.0	0	0	0	0	1	0.00
Totals	9.0	11	8	8	6	7	

Attendance – 40,629, **Game Time** – 3:12

Giants starter Jake Peavy reacts to his pitch during the fourth inning of Game 1 of baseball's NL Division Series in Washington.
AP Photo/Alex Brandon

OCT 3, 2014 NATIONAL PARK

GIANTS 3 • NATIONALS 2

PEAVY PITCHES GIANTS TO 1-0 SERIES LEAD

WASHINGTON, DC

San Francisco Giants GM Brian Sabean traded for Jake Peavy for moments just like this.

The former 2007 NL Cy Young Award winner delivered a gem Friday allowing only two hits over 5 2/3 scoreless innings as the Giants beat the Washington Nationals 3-2 to take a 1-0 lead in the NL Division Series.

It was the first career postseason win for Peavy.

"He mixed really well. He's a very smart pitcher," said catcher Buster Posey, who drove in a run. "He knows when not to give in."

"Nobody is scared of the moment," said Peavy of his new teammates. "We understand that we might not be man for man the favorites, but guys here expect to win."

San Franciscos' Joe Panik steps back into the dugout after scoring on a single by Buster Posey.
AP Photo/Alex Brandon

Giants shortstop Brandon Crawford throws to first on a double play that forced out Nationals' Bryce Harper at second during Game 1 of baseball's NL Division Series.
AP Photo/Alex Brandon

That sentiment is echoed by manager Bruce Bochy who continues his Midas touch in October baseball. The Giants have not lost a postseason game since trailing 3-1 against St. Louis in the NLCS two years ago.

"These guys, they have been through it. They have a calmness about them," Bochy said about his team. "When you have your back as many times against the wall as you can in the postseason, that experience is invaluable."

The first hit Peavy allowed was by Bryce Harper in the fifth, a bouncing single off the glove of diving first baseman Brandon Belt. But any notion of a rally was quickly silenced when Peavy got Wilson Ramos to ground into a first-pitch, 4-6-3 double play, followed by Asdrubal Cabrera's inning-ending foul pop.

Peavy was lifted with two runners aboard in the sixth, and Javier Lopez loaded the bases with a walk. Bochy turned to rookie Hunter Strickland, who promptly took care of Ian Desmond on four fastballs, the last of which hit 100 mph.

"He just stepped into as big a fire as you can step into," Pence said about Strickland, "and he came up huge."

It seems when the lights are brightest, the stage biggest, the stakes highest, these San Francisco Giants come through.

"We've done it so many times now, it seems to be part of our DNA," said Hunter Pence, who stole a base in the fourth and came home on Belt's base hit. "But I think the thing that we know is: What's in the past is in the past, and we've got to move forward and we've got to be ready for the game tomorrow. Because if not, they'll jump all over us."

Giants 3, Nationals 2
October 3, 2014, Nationals Park, Washington, D.C.

	1	2	3	4	5	6	7	8	9	R	H	E
SF	0	0	1	1	0	0	1	0	0	3	12	0
WSH	0	0	0	0	0	0	2	0	0	2	6	0

GIANTS	AB	R	H	RBI	BB	SO	AVG
Blanco CF	4	0	1	0	1	0	.250
Panik 2B	5	1	2	1	0	0	.400
Posey C	4	0	1	1	0	0	.250
Sandoval 3B	5	0	1	0	0	2	.200
Casilla P	0	0	0	0	0	0	---
Pence RF	4	1	1	0	0	0	.250
Belt 1B	4	0	2	1	0	0	.500
Crawford SS	4	0	3	0	0	1	.750
Ishikawa LF	3	1	1	0	0	1	.333
Duffy PH	1	0	0	0	0	0	.000
Romo P	0	0	0	0	0	0	---
Arias 3B	0	0	0	0	0	0	---
Peavy P	2	0	0	0	0	0	.000
Lopez P	0	0	0	0	0	0	---
Strickland P	0	0	0	0	0	0	---
Affeldt P	0	0	0	0	0	0	---
Perez PH-LF	1	0	0	0	0	0	.000
Totals	37	3	12	3	1	4	

2B – Crawford (1, Thornton), 3B – Panik (1, Stammen), RBI – Panik (1), Belt (1), Posey (1), S – Peavy, LOB – 10

NATIONALS	AB	R	H	RBI	BB	SO	AVG
Span CF	4	0	0	0	0	0	.000
Rendon 3B	4	0	1	0	0	0	.250
Werth RF	2	0	0	0	2	1	.000
LaRoche 1B	3	0	1	0	1	1	.333
Desmond SS	4	0	0	0	0	2	.000
Harper LF	4	1	2	1	0	0	.500
Ramos C	3	0	0	0	1	1	.000
Cabrera 2B	4	1	1	1	0	1	.250
Strasburg P	1	0	0	0	0	0	.000
Blevins P	0	0	0	0	0	0	---
Schierholtz PH	1	0	1	0	0	0	1.000
Stammen P	0	0	0	0	0	0	---
Zimmerman PH	1	0	0	0	0	0	.000
Thornton P	0	0	0	0	0	0	---
Clippard P	0	0	0	0	0	0	---
Espinosa PH	1	0	0	0	0	0	---
Totals	32	2	6	2	4	6	

2B – Schierholtz (1, Peavy), HR – Harper (1, 7th inning off Strickland 0 on, 0 Out); Cabrera (1, 7th inning off Strickland 0 on, 1 Out), RBI – Harper (1), Cabrera (1), LOB – 7

GIANTS	IP	H	R	ER	BB	SO	ERA
Peavy (W)	5.2	2	0	0	3	3	0.00
Lopez	0.0	0	0	0	1	0	---
Strickland	1.0	2	2	2	0	2	18.00
Affeldt	0.1	0	0	0	0	0	0.00
Romo	1.0	2	0	0	0	1	0.00
Casilla (S)	1.0	0	0	0	0	0	0.00
Totals	9.0	6	2	2	4	6	

NATIONALS	IP	H	R	ER	BB	SO	ERA
Strasburg (L)	5.0	8	2	1	1	2	1.80
Blevins	1.0	0	0	0	0	1	0.00
Stammen	1.0	2	1	1	0	1	9.00
Thornton	1.0	1	0	0	0	0	0.00
Clippard	1.0	1	0	0	0	0	0.00
Totals	9.0	12	3	2	1	4	

Attendance – 44,035, Game Time – 3:55

Giants starting pitcher Tim Hudson throws in the first inning of Game 2 of baseball's NL Division Series at Nationals Park.
AP Photo/Mark Tenally

GIANTS PREVAIL IN 18

WASHINGTON, DC

Brandon Belt blasted a 94-mph fastball from Washington Nationals reliever Tanner Roark into the second deck in the top of the 18th that was the difference as the Giants edged the Nationals 2-1 for a 2-0 lead in their NL Division Series. It was the 10th consecutive postseason victory for San Francisco.

"I just wanted to get on base for the guys behind me – `Get `em on, get `em over and get `em in.' Fortunately, I put a good enough swing on it," Belt said.

The Giants ran into a buzzsaw in Nationals starting pitcher Jordan Zimmerman, who finished the regular season by throwing a no-hitter and was arguably the hottest pitcher in baseball. Zimmerman had retired 20 batters in a row until walking Giants rookie Joe Panik in the ninth.

Incredibly, Washington manager Matt Williams yanked the hard-

San Franciscos' Brandon Belt watches his solo home run in the 18th inning against the Washington Nationals in Washington.
AP Photo/Patrick Semansky

San Francisco relief pitcher Yusmeiro Petit throws in the 12th inning against Washington.
AP Photo/Patrick Semansky

throwing right hander in favor of Drew Storen who promptly gave up a single to Buster Posey. Down to their final out, the Giants were able to tie it up when Pablo Sandoval doubled allowing Panik to score. Posey was gunned down at the plate preventing the Giants from winning it in the ninth.

Not to be outdone, the Giants Tim Hudson nearly matched Zimmerman pitch for pitch. Hudson went 7 1/3 strong innings giving up seven hits and one earned run.

"That's how we do it. On paper, it might not be the flashiest thing, compared to a lot of teams. But I like this group against anybody in baseball," said Hudson. "Who'd have thought we'd have came here and won the first two?"

The Giants ended up using eight relief pitchers in total but none came up bigger than Yusmeiro Petit who entered in the 12th and threw six scoreless innings, allowing one hit and striking out seven to earn the win.

"I was trying to get as much as I

Giants 2, Nationals 1

October 4, 2014, Nationals Park, Washington, D.C.

	1	2	3	4	5	6	7	8	9	10	11	12	13	14	15	16	17	18	R	H	E
SF	0	0	0	0	0	0	0	0	1	0	0	0	0	0	0	0	0	1	2	8	0
WSH	0	0	1	0	0	0	0	0	0	0	0	0	0	0	0	0	0	0	1	9	0

GIANTS	AB	R	H	RBI	BB	SO	AVG
Blanco CF	6	0	0	0	0	1	.100
Panik 2B	6	1	0	0	1	0	.182
Posey C	6	0	3	0	1	0	.400
Sandoval 3B	7	0	1	1	0	2	.167
Pence RF	7	0	2	0	0	3	.273
Belt 1B	7	1	1	1	0	2	.273
Crawford SS	6	0	0	0	1	2	.300
Ishikawa LF	4	0	1	0	0	0	.286
Affeldt P	0	0	0	0	0	0	---
Casilla P	0	0	0	0	0	0	---
Susac PH	1	0	0	0	0	0	.000
Petit P	1	0	0	0	0	0	.000
Brown PH	1	0	0	0	0	1	.000
Strickland P	0	0	0	0	0	0	---
Hudson P	1	0	0	0	0	1	.000
Machi P	0	0	0	0	0	0	---
Lopez P	0	0	0	0	0	0	---
Duffy PH	1	0	0	0	0	1	.000
Romo P	0	0	0	0	0	0	---
Perez LF	3	0	0	0	1	1	.000
Totals	**57**	**2**	**8**	**2**	**4**	**14**	

NATIONALS	AB	R	H	RBI	BB	SO	AVG
Span CF	7	0	0	0	1	1	.000
Rendon 3B	7	0	4	1	1	1	.455
Werth RF	8	0	1	0	0	2	.100
LaRoche 1B	7	0	0	0	0	2	.100
Desmond SS	6	0	1	0	1	3	.100
Harper LF	7	0	0	0	0	2	.182
Ramos C	7	0	1	0	0	4	.100
Cabrera 2B	4	1	1	0	0	2	.250
Thornton P	0	0	0	0	0	0	---
Barrett P	0	0	0	0	0	0	---
Blevins P	0	0	0	0	0	0	---
Schierholtz PH	0	0	0	0	1	0	1.000
Stammen P	0	0	0	0	0	0	---
Frandsen PH	1	0	0	0	0	0	.000
Soriano P	0	0	0	0	0	0	---
Roark P	1	0	0	0	0	0	.000
Zimmerman P	3	0	0	0	0	2	.000
Storen P	0	0	0	0	0	0	---
Clippard P	0	0	0	0	0	0	---
Zimmerman PH	1	0	1	0	0	0	.500
Espinosa PR-2B	3	0	0	0	0	1	.000
Totals	**62**	**1**	**9**	**1**	**4**	**20**	

2B – Sandoval (1, Storen); Pence (1, Barrett), **HR** – Belt (1, 18th inning off Roark 0 on, 0 Out), **RBI** – Sandoval (1), Belt (2), **S:** Hudson, Blanco, **LOB** – 7

2B – Cabrera (1, Hudson), **RBI** – Rendon (1), **LOB** – 11

GIANTS	IP	H	R	ER	BB	SO	ERA
Hudson	7.1	7	1	1	0	8	1.23
Machi	0.1	0	0	0	0	0	0.00
Lopez	0.1	0	0	0	0	1	0.00
Romo	1.0	0	0	0	0	1	0.00
Affeldt	1.0	1	0	0	0	1	0.00
Casilla	1.0	0	0	0	0	1	0.00
Petit (W)	6.0	1	0	0	3	7	0.00
Strickland (S)	1.0	0	0	0	1	1	9.00
Totals	**18**	**9**	**1**	**1**	**4**	**20**	

NATIONALS	IP	H	R	ER	BB	SO	ERA
Zimmerman	8.2	3	1	1	1	6	1.04
Storen	0.1	2	0	0	0	0	0.00
Clippard	1.0	0	0	0	1	2	0.00
Thornton	1.0	0	0	0	2	1	0.00
Barrett	0.0	1	0	0	0	0	0.00
Blevins	1.0	0	0	0	0	0	0.00
Stammen	3.0	1	0	0	0	1	2.25
Soriano	1.0	0	0	0	0	1	0.00
Roark (L)	2.0	1	1	1	0	3	4.5
Totals	**18**	**8**	**2**	**2**	**4**	**14**	

Attendance – 44,035, **Game Time** – 6:23

could out of him," manager Bruce Bochy said.

Hunter Strickland got the save with a scoreless 18th.

Bochy's Giants, who won the 2010 and 2012 World Series, were built to win this sort of marathon.

"They are relentless. They don't quit," Bochy said. "We had our hands full tonight."

Giants pitcher Madison Bumgarner makes a throw to third for an error that scored two runs in the seventh inning against the Washington Nationals.
AP Photo/Ben Margot

OCT 6, 2014 AT&T PARK

NATIONALS 4 • GIANTS 1

NATIONALS STAY ALIVE WITH 4-1 WIN

SAN FRANCISCO, CALIFORNIA

Doug Fister pitched seven shutout innings and the Washington Nationals capitalized on a Madison Bumgarner error, staving off elimination in the NL Division Series with a 4-1 win over the San Francisco Giants on Monday.

The Nationals cut their deficit to 2-1 in the best-of-five series and in doing so ended the Giants' 10-game postseason winning streak in front of a sellout crowd of 43,627.

Fister's gem left Washington's starters with a 0.87 ERA in the series. The Giants have scored only six runs in all, covering 36 innings.

After Saturday's heart-breaking loss in 18-innings the Nationals needed

Washingtons' Wilson Ramos, right, bunts next to San Franciscos' catcher Buster Posey. Giants pitcher Madison Bumgarner had a throwing error on this play that scored two runs for the Nationals.
AP Photo/Jeff Chiu

Nationals' Ian Desmond, right, slides safely into third base past Giants third baseman Pablo Sandoval, left, before scoring on the same play during the seventh inning of Game 3 of baseball's NL Division Series. At center is third base umpire Brian Knight.
AP Photo/Jeff Chiu

something positive to rally around.

"We just needed one break," Nationals relieve Drew Storen said. "It's been a tough couple innings here to start and we got our break. It's just a matter of building on it, and we live to see another day."

Bumgarner had been nearly untouchable through six, much as he was in the Giants wild-card win over Pittsburgh. But his botched throw in the seventh inning opened the door for the Nationals and prevented the Giants from a three-game sweep.

Ian Desmond singled to start the seventh inning followed by a Bryce Harper walk to bring up Wilson Ramos, who began the season as the

Nationals' cleanup hitter.

Bumgarner fielded Ramos' two-strike sacrifice bunt between the mound and the first-base line and fired to third rather than going for the sure out at first.

"We probably should have taken the out at first. I made a mistake telling him to throw to third," catcher Buster Posey said. "It happens."

Bumgarner's throw sailed wide of Pablo Sandoval's outstretched glove and bounced all the way to the tarp along the left-field wall before rolling over the bullpen mounds where two relievers were warming up.

Sandoval nearly did the splits trying to make the play and stayed down in pain as the two runs scored. Trainers checked on the third baseman and he remained in the game.

When the ball got past Giants left fielder Travis Ishikawa, Harper came all the way around from first and slid into home for the Nationals second run. Asdrubal Cabrera followed with an RBI single to put the Nationals up 3-0.

Harper punctuated the victory with a solo homer in the ninth.

"Being able to get that momentum swing to us a little bit is definitely huge," said Harper, who scored two of the Nationals four runs.

Nationals 4, Giants 1
October 6, 2014, AT&T Park, San Francisco, CA

	1	2	3	4	5	6	7	8	9	R	H	E
WSH	0	0	0	0	0	0	3	0	1	4	7	0
SF	0	0	0	0	0	0	0	1	1	1	6	1

NATIONALS	AB	R	H	RBI	BB	SO	AVG
Span CF	4	0	2	0	0	1	.133
Rendon 3B	4	0	2	0	0	0	.467
Werth RF	4	0	0	0	0	2	.071
LaRoche 1B	4	0	0	0	0	1	.071
Desmond SS	4	1	1	0	0	0	.143
Harper LF	3	2	1	1	1	1	.214
Ramos C	3	1	0	0	0	1	.077
Cabrera 2B	4	0	1	1	0	0	.250
Fister P	3	0	0	0	0	1	.000
Clippard P	0	0	0	0	0	0	---
Schierholtz PH	0	0	0	0	0	0	1.000
Zimmerman PH	1	0	0	0	0	0	.333
Storen P	0	0	0	0	0	0	---
Totals	**34**	**4**	**7**	**2**	**1**	**7**	

HR – Harper (2, 9th inning off Machi 0 on, 0 Out), **RBI** – Cabrera (2), Harper (2), **S** – Ramos, **LOB** – 5

GIANTS	AB	R	H	RBI	BB	SO	AVG
Blanco CF	4	0	0	0	0	0	.071
Panik 2B	4	0	0	0	0	0	.133
Posey C	4	0	1	0	0	1	.357
Sandoval 3B	4	1	2	0	0	0	.250
Pence RF	4	0	1	0	0	0	.267
Belt 1B	3	0	2	0	1	1	.357
Crawford SS	3	0	0	1	0	1	.231
Ishikawa LF	3	0	0	0	1	0	.200
Bumgarner P	1	0	0	0	1	1	.000
Duffy PH	1	0	0	0	0	0	.000
Machi P	0	0	0	0	0	0	---
Affeldt P	0	0	0	0	0	0	---
Totals	**31**	**1**	**6**	**1**	**3**	**4**	

2B – Pence (2, Storen), **RBI** – Crawford (1), **SF** – Crawford, **LOB** – 7

NATIONALS	IP	H	R	ER	BB	SO	ERA
Fister (W)	7.0	4	0	0	3	3	0.00
Clippard	1.0	0	0	0	0	0	0.00
Storen	1.0	2	1	1	0	1	6.75
Totals	**9.0**	**6**	**1**	**1**	**3**	**4**	

GIANTS	IP	H	R	ER	BB	SO	ERA
Bumgarner (L)	7.0	6	3	2	1	6	2.57
Machi	1.2	1	1	1	0	1	4.50
Affeldt	0.1	0	0	0	0	0	0.00
Totals	**9.0**	**7**	**4**	**3**	**1**	**7**	

Attendance – 43,627, **Game Time** – 2:47

OCT 7, 2014 AT&T PARK

GIANTS 3 • NATIONALS 2

GIANTS HEAD BACK TO NLCS

SAN FRANCISCO, CALIFORNIA

You can't accuse this San Francisco Giants team of not taking advantage of their opportunities.

San Francisco is headed back to the National League Championship Series after taking advantage of Washington Nationals reliever Aaron Barrett's bases-loaded wild pitch which allowed the Giants Joe Panik to race home with the deciding run in their 3-2 victory Tuesday night.

With their 3-1 best-of-five Division Series win over the Nationals the Giants continue their remarkable 2014 postseason. They will now square off against the St. Louis Cardinals in a rematch of the 2012 NL Championship Series which the Giants won.

Facing Page: Giants right fielder Hunter Pence makes a leaping catch on a ball hit by Nationals Jayson Werth. *AP Photo/Marcio Jose Sanchez*

Giants starting pitcher Ryan Vogelsong deals in the first inning against the Nationals. *AP Photo/Ben Margot*

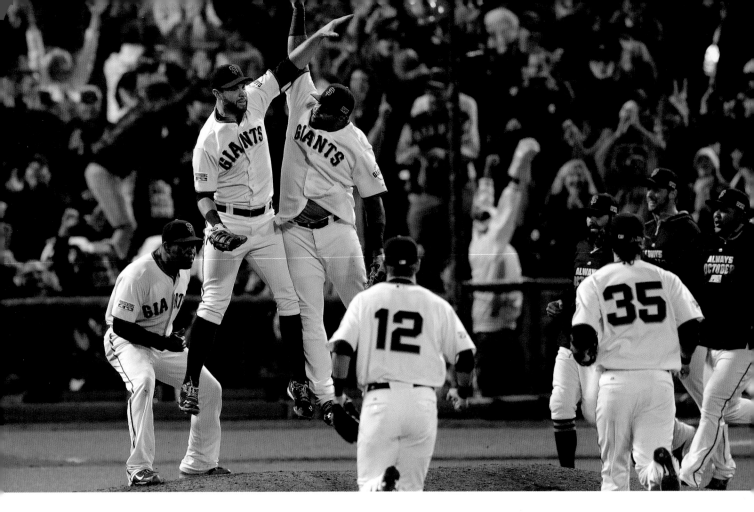

Giants first baseman Brandon Belt, upper left, high fives third baseman Pablo Sandoval and teammates after the Giants beat Washington Nationals in Game 4 of baseball's NL Division Series in San Francisco.
AP Photo/Jeff Chiu

"It's been a remarkable journey. I wouldn't trade it for the world," Giants outfielder Hunter Pence said postgame. "If it was easy, it wouldn't be as fun."

Giants starter Ryan Vogelsong, who hadn't pitched in 11 days, came up big when his team needed it most allowing just two hits over 5 2/3 innings. He has not allowed more than one earned run in five postseason starts dating back to the 2012 NLCS.

"That's as clutch as it comes," Pence said. "It's not an accident that he has the success he does in the playoffs. He's one of those tough, hard-nosed, gritty guys."

San Francisco fans would agree Pence came up clutch as well in the sixth inning as he slammed into the right-field wall robbing Jayson Werth of extra bases.

"That catch he made was unreal. It really brought momentum back in our favor," said Buster Posey.

The Giants struck early against Nationals starter Gio Gonzalez loading the bases in the second. Brandon

Crawford singled and then Juan Perez's slow roller was misplayed by Gonzalez. Vogelsong beat out a bunt single that went untouched and then Blanco drew a four-pitch walk to force home the first run.

Joe Panik followed with a ground out that plated Perez giving the Giants the early one run advantage.

Trailing 2-1 in the seventh, Bryce Harper unloaded on a Hunter Strickland fastball sending it deep into McCovey Cove to tie the game. But in similar fashion to Madison Bumgarner the night before, Barrett threw the game away in the bottom of the seventh.

Panik started the rally in the seventh with a one-out single off Nationals reliever Matt Thornton. After a Posey base hit, Thornton was lifted for Barrett who proceeded to walk Pence to load the bases. Pablo Sandoval stepped to the plate, but never had to swing as Barrett's wild pitch allowed Panik to race home and score.

The Giants will now try to keep their streak of winning in the World Series in even numbered years alive as they look forward to the chance to play again at AT&T Park.

"I think anyone that's here tonight sees what type of electric atmosphere this is, and we just love playing in front of these fans," Posey said.

Giants 3, Nationals 2
October 7, 2014, AT&T Park, San Francisco, CA

	1	2	3	4	5	6	7	8	9	R	H	E
WSH	0	0	0	0	1	0	1	0	0	2	4	1
SF	0	2	0	0	0	0	1	0	-	3	9	0

NATIONALS	AB	R	H	RBI	BB	SO	AVG
Span CF	4	0	0	0	0	1	.105
Rendon 3B	4	0	0	0	0	1	.368
Werth RF	3	0	0	0	1	0	.059
LaRoche 1B	4	0	0	0	0	0	.056
Desmond SS	4	1	1	0	0	1	.167
Harper LF	3	1	2	2	1	0	.294
Ramos C	4	0	1	0	0	0	.118
Cabrera 2B	3	0	0	0	0	2	.200
Gonzalez P	1	0	0	0	0	1	.000
Schierholtz PH	0	0	0	0	1	0	1.000
Roark P	0	0	0	0	0	0	---
Blevins P	0	0	0	0	0	0	---
Zimmerman PH	1	0	0	0	0	0	.250
Thornton P	0	0	0	0	0	0	.000
Barrett P	0	0	0	0	0	0	.000
Soriano P	0	0	0	0	0	0	.000
Totals	31	2	4	2	3	6	

2B – Harper (1, Vogelsong), **HR** – Harper (3, 7th inning off Strickland 0 on, 1 Out), **RBI** – Harper 2 (4), **LOB** – 5

GIANTS	AB	R	H	RBI	BB	SO	AVG
Blanco CF	4	0	1	1	1	0	.111
Panik 2B	4	1	2	1	0	0	.211
Posey C	4	0	2	0	0	0	.389
Pence RF	3	0	1	0	1	0	.278
Sandoval 3B	3	0	0	0	1	0	.211
Belt 1B	4	0	0	0	0	1	.278
Crawford SS	4	1	2	0	0	0	.294
Perez LF	3	1	0	0	0	0	.000
Vogelsong P	2	0	1	0	0	1	.500
Lopez P	0	0	0	0	0	0	---
Duffy PH	1	0	0	0	0	0	.000
Strickland P	0	0	0	0	0	0	---
Romo P	0	0	0	0	0	0	---
Ishikawa PH	1	0	0	0	0	0	.182
Casilla P	0	0	0	0	0	0	---
Totals	33	3	9	2	3	2	

RBI – Blanco (1), Panik (2), **S** – Perez, **LOB** – 10

NATIONALS	IP	H	R	ER	BB	SO	ERA
Gonzalez	4.0	4	2	0	1	1	0.00
Roark	0.2	2	0	0	0	0	3.38
Blevins	1.1	0	0	0	0	1	0.00
Thornton (L)	0.1	2	1	1	0	0	3.86
Barrett	0.1	0	0	0	2	0	0.00
Soriano	1.1	1	0	0	0	0	0.00
Totals	8.0	9	3	1	3	2	

GIANTS	IP	H	R	ER	BB	SO	ERA
Vogelsong	5.2	2	1	1	2	4	1.59
Lopez	0.1	0	0	0	0	0	0.00
Strickland (W)	1.0	2	1	1	0	1	9.00
Romo	1.0	0	0	0	0	0	0.00
Casilla (S)	1.0	0	0	0	1	1	0.00
Totals	9.0	4	2	2	3	6	

Attendance – 43,464, **Game Time** – 3:15

OCT 11, 2014 BUSCH STADIUM

GIANTS 3 • CARDINALS 0

BUMGARNER, SANDOVAL LEAD GIANTS TO GAME 1 VICTORY

ST. LOUIS, MISSOURI

Madison Bumgarner continued his playoff dominance and the San Francisco Giants continued to play winning baseball in October – as usual.

The Giants jumped out to an early two-run lead in the second, which proved to be all they needed as Bumgarner scattered four hits over 7 2/3 scoreless innings as the Giants beat the St. Louis Cardinals 3-0 to take a 1-0 lead in the NL Championship Series.

For those keeping track at home, that's 26 2/3 consecutive shutout in-

Facing Page: Cardinals' Kolten Wong (left) collides with Giants pitcher Madison Bumgarner in a play that resulted in an out at first base in the seventh inning.
AP Photo/St. Louis Post-Dispatch, Huy Mach

San Francisco starting pitcher Madison Bumgarner is congratulated after being taken out of Game 1.
AP Photo/David J. Phillip

Giants' Pablo Sandoval hits a double off St. Louis Cardinals' Adam Wainwright during the second inning of the National League baseball championship series in St. Louis.
AP Photo/Eric Gay

nings on the road by Bumgarner, a new MLB postseason record.

"That's pretty cool," he said. "There's stats for everything nowadays. I've happened to have a little extra good luck on the road."

Make no mistake, Bumgarner hasn't just been lucky—he's been dominant on the road with a 4-0 record and an ERA of 0.59. The lefty and two-time World Series champion was in control in Game 1.

For St. Louis starting pitcher Adam Wainwright and the host Cardinals, luck wasn't in the cards on Saturday. Wainwright failed to complete five innings for the second time in October and made another early exit. The Cardinals' defense had two uncharacteristic and costly mishaps in the second inning and couldn't get things going offensively off of Bumgarner.

"I think there's a scenario out there where I give up one run," Wainwright said. "As ugly as it was, I would say my arm felt better than last time."

Pablo Sandoval led the Giants' offensive attack with three hits including a double to start the two-run second inning. Sandoval scored the first run of the game after a Travis Ishikawa RBI bloop single to left.

"Man, exciting to be in October, you know," Sandoval said. "Last year, I was home watching the game on TV."

With the bases loaded in the second, Cardinals third baseman Matt Carpenter committed a fielding error on a soft one-hop liner by Gregor Blonco. The error was the first of the postseason for the Cardinals.

The Giants' final run came in the third after second baseman Kolten Wong misplayed a double-play ball and Brandon Belt capitalized with a sacrifice fly, making it 3-0 Giants.

"We make a few plays, and we can still be out there playing right now," manager Mike Matheny said.

The Cardinals appeared to gain some momentum in the seventh as Yadier Molina and Jon Jay recorded back-to-back one-out singles, but Wong and pinch hitter Tony Cruz both struck out to end the inning.

The Giants' bullpen came on strong after Bumgarner was taken out in favor of Sergio Romo in the eighth, and Santiago Casilla threw a hitless, scoreless ninth inning for the save.

Giants 3, Cardinals 0

October 11, 2014, Busch Stadium, St. Louis, MO

	1	2	3	4	5	6	7	8	9	R	H	E
SF	0	2	1	0	0	0	0	0	0	3	8	0
STL	0	0	0	0	0	0	0	0	0	0	4	1

GIANTS	AB	R	H	RBI	BB	SO	AVG
Blanco CF	5	0	0	0	0	0	.000
Panik 2B	5	0	1	0	0	0	.200
Posey C	5	1	1	0	0	0	.200
Sandoval 3B	4	1	3	0	1	0	.750
Pence RF	3	1	0	0	1	1	.000
Belt 1B	1	0	1	1	2	0	1.000
Crawford SS	4	0	0	0	0	1	.000
Ishikawa LF	3	0	2	1	0	1	.667
Perez LF	1	0	0	0	0	0	.000
Bumgarner P	4	0	0	0	0	1	.000
Romo P	0	0	0	0	0	0	---
Casilla P	0	0	0	0	0	0	---
Totals	35	3	8	2	4	4	

2B – Sandoval (1, Wainwright), **RBI** – Ishikawa (1), Belt (1), **SF** – Belt, **LOB** – 10

CARDINALS	AB	R	H	RBI	BB	SO	AVG
Carpenter 3B	4	0	1	0	0	1	.250
Grichuk RF	4	0	0	0	0	1	.000
Holliday LF	4	0	0	0	0	0	.000
Peralta SS	3	0	0	0	1	0	.000
Adams 1B	4	0	0	0	0	2	.000
Molina C	4	0	1	0	0	0	.250
Jay CF	2	0	2	0	0	0	1.000
Wong 2B	3	0	0	0	0	1	.000
Wainwright P	1	0	0	0	0	1	.000
Gonzales P	0	0	0	0	0	0	---
Martinez P	0	0	0	0	0	0	---
Choate P	0	0	0	0	0	0	---
Cruz PH	1	0	0	0	0	1	.000
Maness P	0	0	0	0	0	0	---
Totals	30	0	4	0	1	7	

S – Gonzales, **LOB** – 6

GIANTS	IP	H	R	ER	BB	SO	ERA
Bumgarner (W)	7.2	4	0	0	1	7	0.00
Romo	0.1	0	0	0	0	0	0.00
Casilla (S)	1.0	0	0	0	0	0	0.00
Totals	9.0	4	0	0	1	7	

CARDINALS	IP	H	R	ER	BB	SO	ERA
Wainwright (L)	4.2	6	3	2	3	2	3.86
Gonzales	1.1	1	0	0	0	1	0.00
Martinez	0.2	1	0	0	1	1	0.00
Choate	0.1	0	0	0	0	0	0.00
Maness	2.0	0	0	0	0	0	0.00
Totals	9.0	8	3	2	4	4	

Attendance – 47,201, **Game Time** – 3:23

Cardinals' Jon Jay hits a single past San Franciscos' Javier Lopez during the seventh inning in Game 2 of the NLCS.
AP Photo/Eric Gay

OCT 12, 2014 BUSCH STADIUM
CARDINALS 5 • GIANTS 4

WONG'S WALK-OFF EVENS SERIES

ST. LOUIS, MISSOURI

Once again, the St. Louis Cardinals used late game power in the postseason to defeat the San Francisco Giants 5-4 in Game 2 of the National League Championship Series Sunday night.

Cardinals' second baseman Kolten Wong wasted no time in the ninth inning, hitting a leadoff home run that sent the home crowd into a frenzy.

Wong's heroics pushed the Cardinals past the Giants in a back-and-forth game.

The Cardinals Matt Carpenter, Oscar Taveras and Matt Adams also hit home runs in the win. While St. Louis finished dead last in the National League in home runs during the regular season, they have

hit 11 home runs in six postseason games including seven in the seventh inning or later.

As big as the win was for St. Louis,

Giants' Gregor Blanco hits a single in the seventh inning against the Cardinals.
AP Photo/Eric Gay

San Franciscos' Matt Duffy slides safely past Cardinals' Trevor Rosenthal. Duffy scored from second on a wild pitch.
AP Photo/Jeff Roberson

they got some bad news as they are likely without All-Star catcher Yadier Molina for the rest of the way. Molina strained an oblique muscle in the sixth inning.

"We just knew we had to keep grinding," Wong said. "When you lose someone like Yadi, it's definitely tough for us, but we told ourselves we've been going through this all year. Grinding up and down, not getting any easy pass, so we're all so confident."

The Cardinals struck first after Carpenter's home run in the third, followed by a bases loaded RBI single by Randal Grichuk in the fourth to take a 2-0 lead.

After a pinch hit RBI groundout from Joaquin Arias in the fifth and Hunter Pence RBI single in the sixth tied the game, the Giants took a 3-2 lead in the seventh inning following Gregor Blanco's single that scored Brandon Crawford.

Taveras tied the game with a solo home run in the bottom of the seventh. Adams matched that with a solo home run of his own in the eighth.

The Cardinals' lead did not last long. The Giants tied the game on

Cardinals 5, Giants 4

October 12, 2014, Busch Stadium, St. Louis, MO

	1	2	3	4	5	6	7	8	9	R	H	E
SF	0	0	0	0	1	1	1	0	1	4	10	0
STL	0	0	1	1	0	0	1	1	1	5	8	0

GIANTS	AB	R	H	RBI	BB	SO	AVG
Blanco CF	5	0	2	1	0	1	.200
Panik 2B	4	0	1	0	1	1	.222
Posey C	4	0	0	0	1	1	.111
Sandoval 3B	5	1	1	0	0	1	.444
Pence RF	4	0	1	1	0	1	.143
Belt 1B	3	1	1	0	1	1	.500
Crawford SS	3	1	0	0	1	1	.000
Ishikawa LF	2	0	1	0	0	0	.600
Morse PH	1	0	1	0	0	0	1.000
Machi P	0	0	0	0	0	0	---
Lopez P	0	0	0	0	0	0	---
Strickland P	0	0	0	0	0	0	---
Susac PH	1	0	1	0	0	0	1.000
Duffy PR	0	1	0	0	0	0	.000
Romo P	0	0	0	0	0	0	---
Peavy P	1	0	0	0	0	0	.000
Arias PH	1	0	0	1	0	0	.000
Affeldt P	0	0	0	0	0	0	---
Perez PH-LF	1	0	1	0	0	0	.500
Totals	**35**	**4**	**10**	**3**	**4**	**7**	

2B – Ishikawa (1, Lynn); Sandoval (2, Lynn), **RBI** – Arias (1), Pence (1), Blanco (1), **S** – Perez, **LOB** – 9

CARDINALS	AB	R	H	RBI	BB	SO	AVG
Carpenter 3B	4	1	1	1	0	2	.250
Jay CF	4	0	1	0	0	0	.500
Holliday LF	4	0	0	0	0	0	.000
Adams 1B	3	2	1	1	1	0	.143
Peralta SS	2	0	1	0	2	0	.200
Molina C	2	0	1	0	0	0	.333
Cruz C	1	0	0	0	0	1	.000
Wong 2B	3	1	1	1	1	1	.167
Grichuk RF	3	0	1	1	0	0	.143
Lynn P	2	0	0	0	0	1	.000
Choate P	0	0	0	0	0	0	---
Martinez P	0	0	0	0	0	0	---
Taveras PH	1	1	1	1	0	0	1.000
Neshek P	0	0	0	0	0	0	---
Rosenthal P	0	0	0	0	0	0	---
Maness P	0	0	0	0	0	0	---
Totals	**29**	**5**	**8**	**5**	**4**	**5**	

HR – Carpenter (1, 3rd inning off Peavy 0 on, 1 Out); Taveras (1, 7th inning off Machi 0 on, 1 Out); Adams (1, 8th inning off Strickland 0 on, 1 Out); Wong (1, 9th inning off Romo 0 on, 0 Out), **RBI** – Carpenter (1), Grichuk (1), Taveras (1), Adams (1), Wong (1), **S** – Molina, **LOB** – 5

GIANTS	IP	H	R	ER	BB	SO	ERA
Peavy	4.0	4	2	2	3	2	4.50
Affeldt	2.0	0	0	0	1	1	0.00
Machi	0.1	1	1	1	0	0	27.00
Lopez	0.1	1	0	0	0	1	0.00
Strickland	1.1	1	1	1	0	1	6.75
Romo (L)	0.0	1	1	1	0	0	27.00
Totals	**8.0**	**8**	**5**	**5**	**4**	**5**	

CARDINALS	IP	H	R	ER	BB	SO	ERA
Lynn	5.2	6	2	2	1	3	3.18
Choate	0.1	0	1	1	1	1	13.50
Martinez	1.0	2	0	0	0	0	0.00
Neshek	1.0	0	0	0	0	2	0.00
Rosenthal	0.2	2	1	1	2	1	13.50
Maness (W)	0.1	0	0	0	0	0	0.00
Totals	**9.0**	**10**	**4**	**4**	**4**	**7**	

Attendance – 46,262, **Game Time** – 3:41

a wild pitch when Matt Duffy came around to score from second in the ninth inning.

Wong's home run—his second of the postseason—was the deciding factor in Game 2 as the Giants bullpen struggled, allowing home runs in each of the final three innings.

"They are the reason we're in this situation, and you give (the Cardinals) credit," manager Bruce Bochy said. "They threw out some good at-bats and we made a couple of mistakes and they took advantage of them."

San Franciscos' Travis Ishikawa hits a three run double against the St. Louis Cardinals in San Francisco.
AP Photo/Jeff Chiu

OCT 14, 2014 AT&T PARK

GIANTS 5 • CARDINALS 4

WILD THROW AIDS GIANTS' GAME 3 VICTORY

SAN FRANCISCO, CALIFORNIA

Getting a sacrifice bunt down seemed like an impossible task for the San Francisco Giants on Tuesday night.

When they finally did, an errant throw from St. Louis Cardinals reliever Randy Choate in the bottom of the tenth inning allowed Brandon Crawford to score the winning run and give the Giants a 2-1 lead in the NL Championship Series.

Getting the sacrifice bunt down this night was anything but easy.

Crawford drew a leadoff walk in the tenth. After Juan Perez failed two bunt attempts to get Crawford

Giants starting pitcher Tim Hudson celebrates the last out in the top of fifth inning of Game 3 of the NLCS. *AP Photo/Marcio Jose Sanchez*

San Franciscos' Gregor Blanco with the game winning sacrifice bunt during the tenth inning.
AP Photo/Jeff Roberson

to second, he singled instead to bring up another sacrifice situation.

Gregor Blanco struggled on his first bunt attempt as well, fouling it off. But on his second chance he placed a perfect bunt to the left side of the mound, forcing Choate into an inaccurate side-armed throw that

Cardinals second baseman Kolten Wong was unable to snag at first base.

"That's how we decided to win it today," reliever Jeremy Affeldt said with a sly smile. "With this team, you don't necessarily know how it's going to happen. With these two teams playing each other, nothing's scripted."

"We don't do anything easy," Giants manager Bruce Bochy said. "We might have got a little lucky there with Perez when he couldn't get a bunt down and he gets a base hit. But Blanco laid down a beauty.... I don't know if that's luck as much as a great bunt and great speed to put pressure on them."

The Giants got off to a hot start thanks to a three-run double in the first inning from Travis Ishikawa. After that, the Giants had a hard time making any noise. Up until Crawford's walk in the tenth, 16 straight Giants batters were retired.

Wong's triple in the fourth cut the lead in half, scoring Jon Jay and Matt Holliday. A Jhonny Peralta RBI single in the sixth and a solo home run by Randal Grichuk in the seventh knotted the game at 4.

Giants starter Tim Hudson went 6 1/3 innings and struck out five before giving way to the San Francisco bullpen after Grichuk's home run in the seventh.

Reliever Sergio Romo got the win for the Giants.

Giants 5, Cardinals 4
October 14, 2014, AT&T Park, San Francisco, CA

	1	2	3	4	5	6	7	8	9	10	R	H	E
STL	0	0	0	2	0	1	1	0	0	0	4	9	1
SF	4	0	0	0	0	0	0	0	0	1	5	6	0

CARDINALS	AB	R	H	RBI	BB	SO	AVG
Carpenter 3B	5	0	1	0	0	2	.231
Jay CF	5	2	3	0	0	0	.545
Holliday LF	5	1	1	0	0	0	.077
Adams 1B	4	0	0	0	0	0	.091
Peralta SS	4	0	1	1	0	1	.222
Wong 2B	4	0	2	2	0	0	.300
Pierzynski C	4	0	0	0	0	1	.000
Grichuk RF	4	1	1	1	0	2	.182
Lackey P	1	0	0	0	0	1	.000
Descalso PH	1	0	0	0	0	0	.000
Gonzales P	0	0	0	0	0	0	---
Neshek P	0	0	0	0	0	0	---
Maness P	0	0	0	0	0	0	---
Bourjos PH	1	0	0	0	0	2	.000
Choate P	0	0	0	0	0	0	---
Totals	**38**	**4**	**9**	**4**	**0**	**7**	

2B – Wong (1, Hudson), 3B – Wong (1, Hudson), HR – Grichuk (1, 7th inning off Hudson 0 on, 1 Out), RBI – Wong 2 (3), Peralta (1), Grichuk (2), LOB – 5

GIANTS	AB	R	H	RBI	BB	SO	AVG
Blanco CF	4	0	0	0	0	2	.143
Panik 2B	4	0	0	0	0	0	.154
Posey C	4	1	1	0	0	0	.154
Sandoval 3B	3	1	1	0	0	0	.417
Pence RF	4	1	1	1	0	1	.182
Belt 1B	3	1	0	0	1	1	.286
Ishikawa LF	3	0	1	3	0	0	.500
Affeldt P	0	0	0	0	0	0	---
Casilla P	0	0	0	0	0	0	---
Morse PH	1	0	0	0	0	0	.500
Lopez P	0	0	0	0	0	0	---
Romo P	0	0	0	0	0	0	---
Crawford SS	3	1	0	0	1	0	.000
Hudson P	2	0	1	0	0	0	.500
Perez LF	2	0	1	0	0	0	.500
Totals	**33**	**5**	**6**	**4**	**2**	**4**	

2B – Pence (1, Lackey); Ishikawa (2, Lackey), RBI – Pence (2), Ishikawa 3 (4), S – Blanco, LOB – 5

CARDINALS	IP	H	R	ER	BB	SO	ERA
Lackey	6.0	5	4	4	1	3	6.00
Gonzales	1.0	0	0	0	0	1	0.00
Neshek	1.0	0	0	0	0	0	0.00
Maness	1.0	0	0	0	0	0	0.00
Choate (L)	0.0	1	1	0	1	0	13.5
Totals	**9.0**	**6**	**5**	**4**	**2**	**4**	

GIANTS	IP	H	R	ER	BB	SO	ERA
Hudson	6.1	7	4	4	0	5	5.68
Affeldt	1.2	1	0	0	0	0	0.00
Casilla	1.0	0	0	0	0	1	0.00
Lopez	0.2	1	0	0	0	1	0.00
Romo (W)	0.1	0	0	0	0	0	13.50
Totals	**10**	**9**	**4**	**4**	**0**	**7**	

Attendance – 42,716, Game Time – 3:10

Above: Giants' Juan Perez, left, scores past Cardinals catcher A.J. Pierzynski on a hit by Gregor Blanco during Game 4 of the NLCS.
AP Photo/Eric Risberg

Facing Page: San Francisco relief pitcher Yusmeiro Petit throws against St. Louis during the fourth inning.
AP Photo/Jeff Roberson

OCT 15, 2014 AT&T PARK

GIANTS 6 • CARDINALS 4

GIANTS ONE WIN AWAY FROM WORLD SERIES RETURN

SAN FRANCISCO, CALIFORNIA

The saying goes it's better to win ugly than to not win at all.

Style points aside, this San Francisco Giants team continues to find ways to scratch together enough runs to win. Buster Posey knocked in three runs to lead the Giants over the St. Louis Cardinals 6-4 on Wednesday night leaving them with a 3-1 lead in the NL Championship Series and one win away from a return trip to the World Series.

"If you're not hitting the long ball, you have to find ways to manufacture runs," manager Bruce Bochy said.

The Giants did just that.

Trailing 4-3 in the sixth with runners at second and third, Cardinals first baseman Matt Adams fielded Gregor Blanco's grounder but stumbled as he tried to

Giants' Hunter Pence is safe under the tag by Cardinals shortstop Jhonny Peralta after stealing during the fifth inning.
AP Photo/Marcio Jose Sanchez

throw home allowing Juan Perez to score with the tying run.

Joe Panik then hit a sharp grounder right at Adams, who stepped on first base and quickly threw to second for the double play. The throw went wide pulling Cardinals shortstop Jhonny Peralta off the bag and Brandon Crawford, who had been hung up between third and home, broke for the plate and scored easily.

"The play at home, there's a fast runner at third and I was going in on the ball and threw on the run," Adams said. "Just should've made the throw, though. The second one, I should've just touched first and checked home."

Posey followed with a base hit to make it 6-4. The Giants scored three runs in the inning with two of them coming on balls that never left the infield.

"That's kind of fitting of how our postseason's been," Panik said. "It might not be the prettiest way of scoring runs."

"I think any time you can put pressure on the defense, you've got the opportunity for good things to happen," Posey said. "We're able to come up with some big two-out RBIs to get back in the game."

Yusmeiro Petit picked up the win with three scoreless innings in relief of Ryan Vogelsong. Petit has made his mark this postseason having earlier worked six shutout innings in the 18-inning marathon NL Division Series win at Washington.

"He's been really good for us for a long time and he's finally getting some

Giants 6, Cardinals 4

October 15, 2014, AT&T Park, San Francisco, CA

	1	2	3	4	5	6	7	8	9	R	H	E
STL	1	1	2	0	0	0	0	0	0	4	11	0
SF	1	0	2	0	0	3	0	0	–	6	11	0

CARDINALS	AB	R	H	RBI	BB	SO	AVG
Carpenter 3B	4	1	1	0	1	2	.235
Jay CF	3	0	1	0	2	1	.500
Holliday LF	5	1	3	0	0	1	.222
Adams 1B	4	0	2	1	0	0	.200
Peralta SS	4	0	0	0	0	1	.154
Wong 2B	4	2	2	1	0	0	.357
Pierzynski C	2	0	1	1	1	0	.167
Gonzales P	0	0	0	0	0	0	---
Maness P	0	0	0	0	0	0	---
Taveras PH	1	0	1	0	0	0	1.000
Neshek P	0	0	0	0	0	0	.000
Grichuk RF	4	0	0	0	0	2	.133
Miller P	2	0	0	0	0	1	.000
Choate P	0	0	0	0	0	0	---
Martinez P	0	0	0	0	0	0	---
Cruz C	1	0	0	0	0	0	.000
Descalso PH	1	0	0	0	0	0	.000
Totals	**35**	**4**	**11**	**3**	**4**	**8**	

2B – Carpenter (1, Vogelsong); Wong (2, Vogelsong); Holliday (1, Vogelsong), **HR** – Wong (2, 3rd inning off Vogelsong 0 on, 2 Out), **RBI** – Adams (2), Pierzynski (1), Wong (4), **LOB** – 8

GIANTS	AB	R	H	RBI	BB	SO	AVG
Blanco CF	4	2	1	1	1	0	.167
Panik 2B	5	0	1	1	0	0	.167
Posey C	3	1	2	3	1	1	.250
Sandoval 3B	4	0	1	0	1	0	.375
Pence RF	3	0	2	1	1	0	.286
Belt 1B	4	0	1	0	0	1	.273
Ishikawa LF	2	0	0	0	0	1	.400
Perez PH-LF	1	1	0	0	1	1	.400
Crawford SS	3	1	2	0	1	0	.154
Vogelsong P	0	0	0	0	0	0	---
Arias PH	1	1	1	0	0	0	.500
Petit P	1	0	0	0	0	1	.000
Duffy PH	0	0	0	0	0	0	.000
Affeldt P	0	0	0	0	0	0	---
Machi P	0	0	0	0	0	0	---
Lopez P	0	0	0	0	0	0	---
Morse PH	1	0	0	0	0	0	.333
Romo P	0	0	0	0	0	0	---
Casilla P	0	0	0	0	0	0	---
Totals	**32**	**6**	**11**	**6**	**6**	**5**	

2B – Blanco (1, Miller); Crawford (1, Maness), **RBI** – Posey 3 (3), Pence (3), Blanco (2), Panik (1), **S** – Duffy, **SF** – Posey, **LOB** – 10

CARDINALS	IP	H	R	ER	BB	SO	ERA
Miller	3.2	6	3	3	2	3	7.36
Choate	0.1	0	0	0	1	0	9.00
Martinez	1.0	0	0	0	2	0	0.00
Gonzales (L)	0.2	1	3	3	1	0	9.00
Maness	1.1	4	0	0	0	1	0.00
Neshek	1.0	0	0	0	0	1	0.00
Totals	**8.0**	**11**	**6**	**6**	**6**	**5**	

GIANTS	IP	H	R	ER	BB	SO	ERA
Vogelsong	3.0	7	4	4	2	1	12.00
Petit (W)	3.0	1	0	0	1	4	0.00
Affeldt	0.2	0	0	0	1	0	0.00
Machi	0.0	1	0	0	0	0	27.00
Lopez	0.1	0	0	0	0	0	0.00
Romo	1.0	1	0	0	0	1	5.40
Casilla (S)	1.0	1	0	0	0	2	0.00
Totals	**9.0**	**11**	**4**	**4**	**4**	**8**	

Attendance – 43,147, **Game Time** – 3:53

recognition. What a weapon to have," Posey said.

Sergio Romo worked the eighth, and Santiago Casilla finished for his second save of the series. A total of six Giants relievers held St. Louis scoreless over the final six innings.

With a return trip to the World Series in their sights these Giants will continue to do whatever it takes on offense to get a win.

"We might find some weird ways to score runs, but we're getting people on base first. That's the main thing," Brandon Belt said.

Cardinals first baseman Daniel Descalso, left, and Giants' Travis Ishikawa watch Ishikawa's game-winning home run in the ninth inning.
AP Photo/The Sacramento Bee, Randy Pench

OCT 16, 2014 AT&T PARK

GIANTS 6 • CARDINALS 3

ISHIKAWA'S BLAST GIVES GIANTS THE PENNANT

BOBBY THOMSON MUST BE SMILING UP IN HEAVEN

SAN FRANCISCO, CALIFORNIA

In a moment reminiscent of Thomsons' 1951 "Shot Heard 'Round the World", San Francisco Giants left fielder Travis Ishikawa hit a 401 foot walk-off home run in the bottom of the ninth inning to clinch the NL Championship Series, 6-3, over the St. Louis Cardinals and send the Giants on to their third World Series in the last five years.

The unheralded Ishikawa, who started the season in Pittsburgh before being cut and signing with the Giants, knew immediately that he got all of the 2-0 fastball. Raising his right arm triumphantly he took a moment to watch the ball disappear into a sea of orange and black in the right field stands.

"It's gratifying," Ishikawa said. "If

Giants' Joe Panik rounds first after hitting a two-run home run during the third inning of Game 5.
AP Photo/David J. Phillip

Giants' Michael Morse crosses home plate past St. Louis Cardinals catcher Tony Cruz on a game-tying solo home run in the eighth inning.
AP Photo/St. Louis Post Dispatch, Huy Mach

there's an organization I'd want to do it for, it would be this one."

In a move St. Louis fans will be questioning all offseason Cardinals manager Mike Matheny opted to bring in reliever Michael Wacha, who had yet to make an appearance in the postseason, to pitch the ninth.

Pablo Sandoval promptly greeted him with a single to right and after

Hunter Pence flew out, Brandon Belt drew a walk to set the table for Ishikawa's heroics.

"These guys have been through it," Giants manager Bruce Bochy said. "They have been battle-tested and they know how to handle themselves on this type of stage, and then add to that the kids that we brought up, and then Ishikawa."

"I mean, what a great story," Bochy said.

Ishikawa would never have had the chance to be the hero had Michael Morse, pinch hitting for starting pitcher and NLCS MVP Madison Bumgarner, not homered to lead off the eighth inning against Pat Neshek, who had come in for Cardinals starter Adam Wainwright, to even it up 3-3.

"It's unbelievable," Morse said. "This team has been on the same page since the beginning."

Bumgarner was effective once again allowing five hits and three earned runs in eight innings while keeping the Giants in the game. Jeremy Affeldt, pitching for the fourth straight day, earned the win retiring Oscar Taveras on a grounder Affeldt fielded and sprinted over to first for the out.

"Just a gutty effort through all this and I couldn't be prouder of these guys. They just don't stop fighting," Bochy said.

Giants 6, Cardinals 3
October 16, 2014, AT&T Park, San Francisco, CA

	1	2	3	4	5	6	7	8	9	R	H	E
STL	0	0	1	2	0	0	0	0	0	3	6	0
SF	0	0	2	0	0	0	0	1	3	6	7	0

CARDINALS	AB	R	H	RBI	BB	SO	AVG
Carpenter 3B	3	0	0	0	1	1	.200
Jay CF-LF-CF	4	0	2	1	0	0	.500
Holliday LF	4	0	1	0	0	0	.227
Neshek P	0	0	0	0	0	0	---
Wacha P	0	0	0	0	0	0	---
Peralta SS	4	0	0	0	0	0	.118
Adams 1B	3	1	1	1	1	1	.222
Descalso PR-1B	0	0	0	0	0	0	.000
Grichuk RF-LF	4	0	1	0	0	1	.158
Wong 2B	4	0	0	0	0	1	.278
Cruz C	2	2	1	1	2	0	.200
Wainwright P	2	0	0	0	0	1	.000
Bourjos CF	0	0	0	0	0	0	---
Taveras PH-RF	1	0	0	0	0	0	.667
Totals	**31**	**3**	**6**	**3**	**4**	**5**	

2B – Jay (1, Bumgarner), **HR** – Adams (2, 4th inning off Bumgarner 0 on, 0 Out); Cruz (1, 4th inning off Bumgarner 0 on, 2 Out), **RBI** – Jay (1), Adams (3), Cruz (1), **S** – Wainwright, **LOB** – 6

GIANTS	AB	R	H	RBI	BB	SO	AVG
Blanco CF	4	1	2	0	0	0	.227
Panik 2B	4	1	1	2	0	0	.182
Posey C	4	0	0	0	0	1	.200
Sandoval 3B	4	0	2	0	0	1	.400
Arias PR	0	1	0	0	0	0	.500
Pence RF	3	0	0	0	1	1	.235
Belt 1B	3	1	0	0	1	1	.214
Ishikawa LF	3	1	1	3	1	1	.385
Crawford SS	3	0	0	0	0	1	.125
Bumgarner P	2	0	0	0	0	1	.000
Morse PH	1	1	1	1	0	0	.500
Casilla P	0	0	0	0	0	0	---
Affeldt P	0	0	0	0	0	0	---
Totals	**31**	**6**	**7**	**6**	**3**	**7**	

2B – Sandoval (3, Wainwright), **HR** – Panik (1, 3rd inning off Wainwright 1 on, 2 Out); Morse (1, 8th inning off Neshek 0 on, 0 Out); Ishikawa (1, 9th inning off Wacha 2 on, 1 Out), **RBI** – Panik 2 (3), Morse (1), Ishikawa 3 (7) **LOB** – 3

CARDINALS	IP	H	R	ER	BB	SO	ERA
Wainwright	7.0	4	2	2	2	7	3.09
Neshek	1.0	1	1	1	0	0	2.25
Wacha (L)	0.1	2	3	3	1	0	81.00
Totals	**8.1**	**7**	**6**	**6**	**3**	**7**	

GIANTS	IP	H	R	ER	BB	SO	ERA
Bumgarner	8.0	5	3	3	2	5	1.72
Casilla	0.2	1	0	0	2	0	0.00
Affeldt (W)	0.1	0	0	0	0	0	0.00
Totals	**9.0**	**6**	**3**	**3**	**4**	**5**	

Attendance – 43,217, **Game Time** – 3:03

San Francisco Giants celebrate after a walk-off three-run home run during the ninth inning of Game 5 of the NLCS.
(AP Photo/Ben Margot)

OCT 21, 2014 KAUFFMAN STADIUM

GIANTS 7 • ROYALS 1

BUMGARNER DOMINATES AS GIANTS TAKE 1-0 LEAD

KANSAS CITY, MISSOURI

The Kansas City Royals had heard the praise for Madison Bumgarner throughout the 2014 postseason. On Tuesday night in Kansas City, they found out Bumgarner was every bit as good as advertised.

The Giants dominating left-hander pitched three-hit ball for seven innings as San Francisco rolled to a 7-1 win over Kansas City in the World Series opener. It was the Giants seventh consecutive World Series game win while the Royals suffered their first

Above: Royals catcher Salvador Perez (13) tags Giants catcher Buster Posey (28) just in time for the out as the home plate umpire watches.
Sportswire via AP Images

Facing Page: Giants pitcher Madison Bumgarner throws during the first inning.
AP Photo/Jamie Squire, Pool

San Franciscos' Pablo Sandoval hits an RBI single during the seventh inning against the Kansas City Royals.
AP Photo/Jeff Roberson

Pitcher Madison Bumgarner makes a play from his knees on a ball hit by Kansas City Royals' Eric Hosmer during the sixth inning.
AP Photo/David J. Phillip

loss this postseason.

The 25-year-old left-hander faced only one serious threat from the Royals in the third inning. The Royals loaded the bases with a two-out walk but cleanup man Eric Hosmer grounded out on the first pitch to end the inning.

Bumgarner improved to 3-0 in World Series play and extended his scoreless streak to 21 innings before the Royals Salvador Perez homered with two outs in the seventh.

"I would tell you I wasn't thinking about it, but you know," Bumgarner said. "There's no way around it. There's so much talk about it. Obviously, a World Series game is not something you tend to forget."

"The Royals have obviously been

Giants third baseman Pablo Sandoval blows bubble gum during Game 1 of baseball's World Series.
AP Photo/Matt Slocum

on a great run. You don't get here without that," Bumgarner said. "I think our team is concentrating on what they need to do, not what the Royals are doing."

For Royals starter James Shields this was a night he might want to forget. Looking tight from the start Shields struggled with his command.

After a bloop single by Gregor Blanco and a line drive base hit by Buster Posey, Pablo Sandoval stepped up and doubled to right bringing home Blanco with the Giants first run. The Royals caught a break on the play as Posey was gunned down at the plate on a perfect relay from Norichika Aoki for the second out.

Shields, however, couldn't get out of the inning without further damage.

Hunter Pence homered to center field giving the Giants a 3-0 lead before the Royals home crowd had a chance to get settled in their seats.

By the time Shields struck out Michael Morse to end the first, he had thrown 32 pitches.

"It just wasn't my night tonight," Shields said. "We're ready to move on tomorrow. We have a lot of positive attitude right now, we're tracking at an all-time high. We just faced a good pitcher tonight."

Coming into the game the Royals knew runs would be tough to come by against the Giants ace.

The Royals will now attempt to battle back against the odds — the Game 1 winner has won 15 of the last 17 World Series

"We didn't expect to come in here and sweep the San Francisco Giants," Kansas City manager Ned Yost said.

Facing Page: San Franciscos' third baseman Pablo Sandoval and teammate Brandon Belt celebrate following their 7-1 victory over the Kansas City Royals. *AP Photo/Matt Slocum*

Giants 7, Royals 1
October 21, 2014, Kauffman Stadium, Kansas City, MO

	1	2	3	4	5	6	7	8	9	R	H	E
SF	3	0	0	2	0	0	2	0	0	7	11	1
KC	0	0	0	0	0	0	1	0	0	1	4	0

GIANTS	AB	R	H	RBI	BB	SO	AVG
Blanco CF	3	2	1	1	2	0	.333
Panik 2B	5	1	1	1	0	1	.200
Posey C	5	0	1	0	0	0	.200
Sandoval 3B	5	1	3	2	0	0	.600
Pence RF	3	2	2	2	2	0	.667
Belt 1B	4	1	1	0	1	2	.250
Morse DH	5	0	1	1	0	3	.200
Ishikawa LF	1	0	0	0	0	0	.000
Perez PH-LF	2	0	0	0	0	1	.000
Crawford SS	3	0	1	0	1	0	.333
Totals	**36**	**7**	**11**	**7**	**6**	**7**	

2B – Sandoval (1, Shields); Pence (1, Shields), **3B** – Panik (1, Duffy), **HR** – Pence (1, 1st inning off Shields 1 on, 2 Out), **RBI** – Sandoval 2 (2), Pence 2 (2), Morse (1), Blanco (1), Panik (1), **S** – Perez, **LOB** – 9

ROYALS	AB	R	H	RBI	BB	SO	AVG
Escobar SS	4	0	1	0	0	1	.250
Aoki RF	4	0	0	0	0	1	.000
Cain CF	2	0	0	0	1	1	.000
Hosmer 1B	4	0	0	0	0	0	.000
Butler DH	3	0	1	0	0	0	.333
Willingham PH	1	0	0	0	0	1	.000
Gordon LF	3	0	0	0	0	1	.000
Perez C	3	1	1	1	0	1	.333
Infante 2B	3	0	0	0	0	0	.000
Moustakas 3B	3	0	1	0	0	1	.333
Totals	**30**	**1**	**4**	**1**	**1**	**7**	

2B – Moustakas (1, Bumgarner), **HR** – Perez (1, 7th inning off Bumgarner 0 on, 2 Out), **RBI** – Perez (1), **LOB** – 4

GIANTS	IP	H	R	ER	BB	SO	ERA
Bumgarner (W)	7.0	3	1	1	1	5	1.29
Lopez	1.0	1	0	0	0	0	0.00
Strickland	1.0	0	0	0	0	2	0.00
Totals	**9.0**	**4**	**1**	**1**	**1**	**7**	

ROYALS	IP	H	R	ER	BB	SO	ERA
Shields (L)	3.0	7	5	5	1	1	15.00
Duffy	3.0	1	2	2	3	3	6.00
Collins	2.0	2	0	0	1	2	0.00
Frasor	1.0	1	0	0	1	1	0.00
Totals	**9.0**	**11**	**7**	**7**	**6**	**7**	

Attendance – 40,459, **Game Time** – 3:32

San Francisco Giants Pablo Sandoval tags up at second base after hitting a double during the World Series against the Kansas City Royals.
AP Photo/Charlie Neibergall

OCT 22, 2014 KAUFFMAN STADIUM

ROYALS 7 • GIANTS 2

ROYALS FIGHT BACK EVEN SERIES 1-1

KANSAS CITY, MISSOURI

Billy Butler knew the Kansas City Royals needed a spark. After getting dominated by San Francisco Giants ace Madison Bumgarner in Game 1 and falling behind 1-0 in the top of the first inning in Game 2, the Royals fan who had packed Kauffman Stadium were looking for something to cheer about.

Butler provided just that in the bottom half of the first by lining a fastball from Giants starter Jake Peavy in to left center that plated Lorenzo

Cain. The Royals stranded Eric Hosmer at third but the message was sent – these Royals weren't

San Franciscos' catcher Buster Posey talks with Jake Peavy before Peavy was relieved by Jean Machi.
AP Photo/Charlie Neibergall

Royals shortstop Alcides Escobar attempts to steal second, but is tagged out by Giants second baseman Joe Panik in the first inning of baseball's World Series, in Kansas City, Mo.
AP Photo/The Sacramento Bee, Paul Kitagaki Jr.

going down without a fight.

"We showed them that we have fight in us, and I think they knew that already," said Billy Butler, whose RBI single in the sixth inning gave the Royals a 3-2 lead. "But we stepped up big there as a team, and that gave us some confidence."

"With their pitching and our pitching, and the way both teams play, we're going to have a fight, I think, every game," Giants manager Bruce Bochy said.

In the second inning the Royals went right back to work as Omar Infante doubled over the head of Travis Ishikawa in left field, and Alcides Escobar delivered a two-out double down the right-field line to give Kansas City a 2-1 lead.

San Franciscos' left fielder Travis Ishikawa dives for a double hit by Kansas City Royals' Lorenzo Cain in the first inning of Game 2.
AP Photo/The Sacramento Bee, Paul Kitagaki Jr.

The Giants answered right back.

Brandon Belt tied it in the fourth with a double that bounced off Nori Aoki's glove in right field scoring Pablo Sandoval, who had doubled to lead off the inning.

With the game still tied at two in the bottom of the sixth the Royals rallied.

After the Royals got their first two batters aboard Giants manager Bochy decided to pull Peavy for Jean Machi. Butler greeted Machi with a go-ahead single. Lefty Javier Lopez was brought in to face Alex Gordon, who he got to fly out to left for the first out. Bochy then turned to Hunter Strickland to pitch to Salvador Perez.

Perez fell behind 0-2 before Strickland's wild pitch allowed Terrance Gore and Eric Hosmer to move up to second and third. Down 1-2 in the count, Perez drilled a

First baseman Brandon Belt lies on the infield after being tagged out at second to end the top of the fourth inning.
AP Photo/The Sacramento Bee, Paul Kitagaki Jr.

fastball in to the gap for a two-run double as the Kansas City fans erupted.

When Omar Infante followed with a home run to left, an angry Strickland got into a shouting match with Perez as the Royals catcher trotted home. Strickland shouted at Perez, Perez shouted back at Strickland. Players from both teams charged out of their dugouts before the umpires finally restored order.

"He started to look at me, so I asked him like, 'Hey, why you look at me?'" Perez said. "So he was telling me, 'Get out of here, whatever.' So I don't know. You don't have to treat me like that. Look at Omar. Omar hit a bomb. I

Giants' Michael Morse breaks his bat on a foul ball during Game 2.
AP Photo/David J. Phillip

didn't hit a bomb. I hit a double."

Strickland said he simply let his frustration get to him.

"I let the team down," he said. "My emotions got to me."

The Royals Yordano Ventura kept the Giants bats at bay through six strong innings. The hard-throwing 23-year old settled down after Giants Gregor Blanco lead off the game with a home run. He gave up eight hits and two earned runs.

The dynamic trio of Kelvin Herrera, Wade Davis and Greg Holland did the rest shutting out the Giants in the final three innings – just as they have done to teams all season.

"For us to leave here with a split, you like to get greedy," Bochy said, "but we know it's going to be a tough series."

Giants relief pitcher Hunter Strickland reacts after Royals' Salvador Perez said something to Strickland following a two run home run by Omar Infante. *AP Photo/The Sacramento Bee, Paul Kitagaki Jr.*

Royals 7, Giants 2
October 22, 2014, Kauffman Stadium, Kansas City, MO

	1	2	3	4	5	6	7	8	9	R	H	E
SF	1	0	0	1	0	0	0	0	0	2	9	0
KC	1	1	0	0	0	5	0	0	–	7	10	0

GIANTS	AB	R	H	RBI	BB	SO	AVG
Blanco CF	4	1	1	1	1	1	.286
Panik 2B	4	0	1	0	0	0	.222
Posey C	4	0	1	0	0	1	.222
Sandoval 3B	4	1	1	0	0	1	.444
Pence RF	4	0	1	0	0	1	.429
Belt 1B	4	0	1	1	0	1	.250
Morse DH	3	0	1	0	0	0	.250
Susac PH	1	0	0	0	0	1	.000
Ishikawa LF	4	0	1	0	0	2	.200
Crawford SS	3	0	1	0	1	0	.333
Totals	**35**	**2**	**9**	**2**	**2**	**8**	

2B – Sandoval (2, Ventura); Belt (1, Ventura), **HR** – Blanco (1, 1st inning off Ventura 0 on, 0 Out), **RBI** – Blanco (2), Belt (1), **LOB** – 8

ROYALS	AB	R	H	RBI	BB	SO	AVG
Escobar SS	4	0	2	1	0	1	.375
Aoki RF	3	0	0	0	0	0	.000
Dyson CF	1	0	0	0	0	0	.000
Cain CF-RF	4	2	2	0	0	0	.333
Hosmer 1B	2	1	0	0	2	1	.000
Butler DH	3	0	2	2	0	0	.500
Gore PR-DH	0	1	0	0	0	0	.000
Willingham PH-DH	1	0	0	0	0	1	.000
Gordon LF	4	0	0	0	0	0	.000
Perez C	4	1	1	2	0	1	.286
Infante 2B	3	2	2	2	0	0	.333
Moustakas 3B	3	0	1	0	0	0	.333
Totals	**32**	**7**	**10**	**7**	**2**	**4**	

2B – Cain (1, Peavy); Infante (1, Peavy); Escobar (1, Peavy); Perez (1, Strickland), **HR** – Infante (1, 6th inning off Strickland 1 on, 1 Out), **RBI** – Butler 2 (2), Escobar (1), Perez 2 (3), Infante 2 (2), **LOB** – 3

GIANTS	IP	H	R	ER	BB	SO	ERA
Peavy (L)	5.0	6	4	4	2	1	7.20
Machi	0.0	1	1	1	0	0	INF
Lopez	0.1	0	0	0	0	0	0.00
Strickland	0.0	2	2	2	0	0	18.00
Affeldt	0.2	1	0	0	0	0	0.00
Lincecum	1.2	0	0	0	0	2	0.00
Casilla	0.1	0	0	0	0	1	0.00
Totals	**8.0**	**10**	**7**	**7**	**2**	**4**	

ROYALS	IP	H	R	ER	BB	SO	ERA
Ventura	5.1	8	2	2	0	2	3.38
Herrera (W)	1.2	0	0	0	2	1	0.00
Davis	1.0	0	0	0	0	2	0.00
Holland	1.0	1	0	0	0	3	0.00
Totals	**9.0**	**9**	**2**	**2**	**2**	**8**	

Attendance – 40,446, **Game Time** – 3:25

OCT 24, 2014 AT&T PARK

ROYALS 3 • GIANTS 2

ROYALS USE FAMILIAR RECIPE TO TAKE WORLD SERIES LEAD

SAN FRANCISCO, CALIFORNIA

The Kansas City Royals used a familiar recipe to win Game 3 of the World Series.

Run-saving defense, timely hitting and stellar late-inning relief led the Royals to a 3-2 win to move ahead in the Series, two games to one, with their second consecutive victory.

"It was a tight ballgame," said Giants manger Bruce Bochy, who made it clear afterward he would not bring back Game 1 starter Madison Bumgarner on short rest

First baseman Travis Ishikawa catches a fly ball by Kansas City Royals Salvador Perez.
AP Photo/Jeff Chiu

Facing Page: Giants pitcher Tim Hudson throws during the first inning of Game 3.
AP Photo/Paul Buck, Pool

Above: Giants' Brandon Crawford singles during the sixth inning of Game 3 in San Francisco.
AP Photo/Charlie Riedel

Facing Page: Michael Morse hits an RBI double during the sixth inning against the Kansas City Royals.
AP Photo/Charlie Riedel

just because his club trailed in the Series.

"Both sides pitched well. They just pitched a little better than we did. It always comes down to pitching."

It was the kind of game the Royals won time after time down the stretch to get to the playoffs as well as during the first three postseason rounds when they went 8-0.

"This is the way our games have gone all year," said Royals manager Ned Yost. "I'm getting really good at protecting a one-run lead because a lot of times that's exactly what we have to deal with.

"But I have the necessary tools to be able to do that. It's not me doing it. We have the type of pitchers in our bullpen that can accomplish that."

Giants Hunter Pence is tagged out attempting to steal second base by Royals shortstop Alcides Escobar.
AP Photo/Jeff Chiu

Much was made before the game about San Francisco's Tim Hudson finally getting his chance to pitch in a World Series game after 457 career starts, the longest wait of any active pitcher. But the 39-year-old righty was rudely greeted to the big stage when his first pitch of the game was smashed to deep left by Alcides Escobar for a double.

The Royals then did what they do best offensively – play small ball. Alex Gordon grounded out to second, moving Escobar to third, and Lorenzo Cain scored him with a grounder to short for a quick 1-0 lead.

Lorenzo Cain, moved to right field by Yost, continued to shine defensively. Cain robbed Buster Posey of a hit in the first inning with a sliding catch in the gap and turned away Travis Ishikawa's bid for a hit in the second with a sliding catch toward the line.

Hudson appeared ready to crack early when Mike Moustakas led off the second inning with a single and Omar Infante drew a walk. But Ishikawa – a first baseman playing left field out of necessity – gave Hudson a big lift by making a sliding catch toward the line to rob Salvador Perez of a hit.

Hudson then did something that's not easy to do – get the speedy Jarrod Dyson to ground into a double play.

Escaping that jam settled down Hudson, who proceeded to retire 12 consecutive hitters. That string came to an end when Escobar singled up the middle with one down in the sixth inning and raced around to score on Gordon's booming double to center.

With two down, Bochy summoned lefty Javy Lopez to face Eric Hosmer, who put a tremendous at-bat on him. Hosmer stayed alive for 11 pitches fouling off four two-strike offerings before smacking an RBI single up the middle to make it 3-0.

Brandon Crawford led off the sixth with a single and scored on pinch-hitter Michael Morse's double, prompting Yost to lift Guthrie for hard-throwing Kelvin Herrera.

With his velocity down a few clicks and his command off, Herrera walked Gregor Blanco on four pitches. He got the next three hitters to ground out, however, with Posey's knocking in a run to make it 3-2.

"My mind set is I'm not going to get beat in the sixth inning with the bullpen I've got," said Yost. "I just wasn't going to take any chances. It's a big game. It's a pivotal game, in my mind."

Right fielder Hunter Pence catches a fly ball by Kansas City Royals Lorenzo Cain.
AP Photo/Matt Slocum

It took both Herrera and rookie Brandon Finnegan for the Royals to navigate through the seventh inning. That put them right where they wanted to be, with a lead and Wade Davis ready for the eighth and Greg Holland the ninth.

"It's a tough one to swallow. It was a hard-fought game on both sides, like everybody probably anticipated," Hudson said. "We just came up a little short. They just did the little things they needed to beat us."

A fan holds a sign for Hunter Pance during the World Series between the Kansas City Royals and the San Francisco Giants in San Francisco.
AP Photo/Charlie Riedel

Royals 3, Giants 2
October 24, 2014, AT&T Park, San Francisco, CA

	1	2	3	4	5	6	7	8	9	R	H	E
KC	1	0	0	0	0	2	0	0	0	3	6	0
SF	0	0	0	0	0	2	0	0	0	2	4	0

ROYALS	AB	R	H	RBI	BB	SO	AVG
Escobar SS	4	2	2	0	0	1	.417
Gordon LF	4	1	1	1	0	1	.091
Cain RF	4	0	0	1	0	0	.200
Hosmer 1B	4	0	1	1	0	1	.100
Moustakas 3B	4	0	1	0	0	1	.300
Infante 2B	3	0	0	0	1	2	.222
Perez C	3	0	0	0	0	0	.200
Dyson CF	3	0	1	0	0	0	.250
Guthrie P	2	0	0	0	0	0	.000
Herrera P	1	0	0	0	0	1	.000
Finnegan P	0	0	0	0	0	0	---
Davis P	0	0	0	0	0	0	---
Holland P	0	0	0	0	0	0	---
Totals	**32**	**3**	**6**	**3**	**1**	**7**	

2B – Escobar (2, Hudson); Gordon (1, Hudson), **RBI** – Cain (1), Gordon (1), Hosmer (1), **LOB** – 3

GIANTS	AB	R	H	RBI	BB	SO	AVG
Blanco CF	3	0	0	0	1	0	.200
Panik 2B	4	0	0	0	0	1	.154
Posey C	4	0	0	1	0	0	.154
Sandoval 3B	4	0	0	0	0	0	.308
Pence RF	3	0	1	0	1	0	.400
Belt 1B	3	0	1	0	0	1	.273
Ishikawa LF	2	0	0	0	0	0	.143
Perez PH-LF	1	0	0	0	0	0	.000
Crawford SS	3	1	1	0	0	1	.333
Affeldt P	0	0	0	0	0	0	---
Casilla P	0	0	0	0	0	0	---
Hudson P	1	0	0	0	0	0	.000
Lopez P	0	0	0	0	0	0	---
Morse PH	1	1	1	1	0	0	.333
Romo P	0	0	0	0	0	0	---
Arias SS	1	0	0	0	0	1	.000
Totals	**30**	**2**	**4**	**2**	**2**	**4**	

2B – Morse (1, Guthrie), **RBI** – Morse (2), Posey (1), **LOB** – 3

ROYALS	IP	H	R	ER	BB	SO	ERA
Guthrie (W)	5.0	4	2	2	0	0	3.60
Herrera	1.1	0	0	0	2	1	0.00
Finnegan	0.2	0	0	0	0	1	0.00
Davis	1.0	0	0	0	0	2	0.00
Holland (S)	1.0	0	0	0	0	0	0.00
Totals	**9.0**	**4**	**2**	**2**	**2**	**4**	

GIANTS	IP	H	R	ER	BB	SO	ERA
Hudson (L)	5.2	4	3	3	1	2	4.76
Lopez	0.1	1	0	0	0	1	0.00
Romo	1.1	1	0	0	0	3	0.00
Affeldt	1.1	0	0	0	0	0	0.00
Casilla	0.1	0	0	0	0	1	0.00
Totals	**9.0**	**6**	**3**	**3**	**1**	**7**	

Attendance – 43,020, **Game Time** – 3:15

OCT 25, 2014 AT&T PARK

GIANTS 11 • ROYALS 4

GIANTS RALLY PAST ROYALS TO EVEN WORLD SERIES

SAN FRANCISCO, CALIFORNIA

The sixth inning has been fraught with peril for both clubs in the World Series, so it was no accident that Kansas City manager Ned Yost was asked about it before Game 4.

"I feel it's one of the most important innings of the game for us," said Yost, whose club had scored seven runs in that frame in the previous two games. "It's been like that for a while.

"We feel we have the seventh, eighth and ninth covered. Sometimes, we've got to mix and match in the sixth."

Facing Page: Relief pitcher Yusmeiro Petit delivers a pitch in the fourth inning of Game 4.
Icon Sportswire via AP Images

Above: Giants' Joe Panik hits a two-run RBI double during the seventh inning of Game 4.
AP Photo/Charlie Riedel

Center fielder Gregor Blanco catches a deep fly ball near the wall, as right fielder Hunter Pence watches.
Icon Sportswire via AP Images

It wasn't so much mixing and matching Saturday night as slicing and dicing, courtesy of San Francisco's offense. By scoring three runs to take a 7-4 lead, the Giants never had to face the Royals standout late-inning relief trio of Kelvin Herrera, Wade Davis and Greg Holland.

What became an 11-4 romp at rocking AT&T Park also gave this entertaining World Series a dramatic turn in favor of the Giants. Instead of falling behind, three games to one, they drew even with postseason ace Madison Bumgarner set to pitch on regular rest in Game 5.

Pablo Sandoval celebrates while standing at first base with first base coach Roberto Kelly after hitting a two-run RBI single during the sixth inning of Game 4.
AP Photo/Jeff Chiu

"This was a great ballgame, I thought, especially the way we came back," Giants manager Bruce Bochy said.

Yost was able to get to his three lock-down relievers with leads in the previous two games but not in this one. Given a 4-2 lead after three innings,

starting pitcher Jason Vargas was yanked after allowing a leadoff double to Joe Panik in the bottom of the fifth.

Yost went to right-hander Jason Frasor and lefty Danny Duffy in that inning but they were unable to prevent the Giants from drawing even. Hunter Pence knocked in the first run with

San Franciscos' Gregor Blanco slides into home plate as Kansas Citys' Salvador Perez waits for the throw on a two-run RBI double by Joe Panik.
AP Photo/Matt Slocum

a single off Frasor and Juan Perez delivered the other off Duffy with a sacrifice fly to centerfielder Jarrod Dyson, whose diving catch prevented more damage.

With the score tied and momentum in the World Series on the line, Yost turned the sixth inning over to lefty Brandon Finnegan, who back in June was pitching for TCU in the College World Series.

Nothing went right for young

Finnegan, beginning with Joaquin Arias' pinch-hit single to open the inning. The Royals even lost the first video replay challenge in World Series history, a pickoff play at second base that left the Giants with two on and no outs.

Pablo Sandoval, a .199 hitter right-handed during the regular season, would come through from that side for the second time in the game with a two-run, two-out single that snapped

Giants' Hunter Pence makes a diving catch on a ball hit by Royals' Lorenzo Cain during the ninth inning.
AP Photo/Eric Risberg

the 4-4 tie. Brandon Belt, batting lefty on lefty, followed with an RBI single to give the Giants a three-run lead and the rout was on.

"He's just a clutch hitter," Yost said of Sandoval. "We had cut a run down at the plate and I thought we had the situation in the palm of our hand. He did a great job of hitting the ball up the middle. It was a great at-bat. It won the ball game for them."

"We never give up, that's the thing," said Sandoval, who shook off a stomach bug after starting to feel ill

Friday. "We've been doing it all year in these situations. We know how that fccls."

While Kansas City's middle relief struggled, San Francisco's Yusmeiro Petit did his usual job of calming things down after the Royals jumped to an early 4-2 lead off Ryan Vogelsong. Petit pitched three shutout innings, allowing only two hits and setting the stage for the Giants' comeback.

So, the Giants' decision not to panic and pitch Bumgarner on short

Juan Perez makes a catch on a hit by Kansas City Royals' Alex Gordon.
AP Photo/Marcio Jose Sanchez

Giants 11, Royals 4

October 25, 2014, AT&T Park, San Francisco, CA

	1	2	3	4	5	6	7	8	9	R	H	E
KC	0	0	4	0	0	0	0	0	0	4	12	1
SF	1	0	1	0	2	3	4	0	–	11	16	0

ROYALS	AB	R	H	RBI	BB	SO	AVG
Escobar SS	5	0	1	0	0	1	.353
Gordon LF	5	1	1	0	0	1	.125
Cain RF	5	1	2	0	0	1	.267
Hosmer 1B	5	1	3	1	0	1	.267
Moustakas 3B	3	1	0	0	1	0	.231
Collins P	0	0	0	0	0	0	---
Infante 2B	4	0	1	2	0	1	.231
Perez C	4	0	3	1	0	0	.357
Dyson CF	3	0	1	0	1	0	.286
Vargas P	2	0	0	0	0	1	.000
Frasor P	0	0	0	0	0	0	---
Duffy P	0	0	0	0	0	0	---
Aoki PH	1	0	0	0	0	0	.000
Finnegan P	0	0	0	0	0	0	---
Nix 3B	1	0	0	0	0	1	.000
Totals	**38**	**4**	**12**	**4**	**2**	**7**	

2B – Hosmer (1, Petit); Gordon (2, Strickland), **RBI** – Hosmer (2), Infante 2 (4), Perez (4), **LOB** – 9

ROYALS	IP	H	R	ER	BB	SO	ERA
Vargas	4.0	6	3	3	2	3	6.75
Frasor	0.1	1	1	1	0	0	6.75
Duffy	0.2	1	0	0	1	1	4.91
Finnegan (L)	1.0	5	5	5	2	0	27.00
Collins	2.0	3	2	2	1	2	4.50
Totals	**8.0**	**16**	**11**	**11**	**6**	**6**	

Attendance – 43,066, **Game Time** – 4:00

GIANTS	AB	R	H	RBI	BB	SO	AVG
Blanco CF	5	3	2	0	1	0	.267
Panik 2B	4	2	2	2	0	0	.235
Posey C	3	1	1	1	2	0	.188
Pence RF	5	2	3	3	0	0	.467
Sandoval 3B	5	0	2	2	0	2	.333
Belt 1B	3	0	1	1	2	1	.286
Perez LF	4	0	1	1	0	1	.143
Crawford SS	5	1	1	0	0	2	.286
Vogelsong P	0	0	0	0	0	0	---
Machi P	0	0	0	0	0	0	---
Duffy PH	1	1	1	0	0	0	1.000
Petit P	1	0	1	0	0	0	1.000
Arias PH	1	0	1	0	0	0	.500
Affeldt P	0	0	0	0	0	0	---
Morse PH	0	1	0	0	1	0	.333
Romo P	0	0	0	0	0	0	---
Ishikawa PH	1	0	0	0	0	0	.125
Strickland P	0	0	0	0	0	0	---
Totals	**38**	**11**	**16**	**10**	**6**	**6**	

2B – Panik 2 (2, Vargas, Collins); Pence (2, Collins), **RBI** – Pence 3 (5), Posey (2), Perez (1), Sandoval 2 (4), Belt (2), Panik 2 (3), **S** – Panik, **SF** – Perez, **LOB** – 11

GIANTS	IP	H	R	ER	BB	SO	ERA
Vogelsong	2.2	7	4	4	1	2	13.50
Machi	0.1	0	0	0	1	1	27.00
Petit (W)	3.0	2	0	0	0	2	0.00
Affeldt	1.0	1	0	0	0	0	0.00
Romo	1.0	1	0	0	0	1	0.00
Strickland	1.0	1	0	0	0	1	9.00
Totals	**9.0**	**12**	**4**	**4**	**2**	**7**	

rest was looking like pure genius by the end of the long night. It hardly mattered that starting pitcher Vogelsong was cuffed around for four runs in 22/3 innings, with some suspect infield defense playing a role.

So, it would appear to be advantage Giants with their ace set to go Sunday.

"This was really big, no doubt about it," said Giants catcher Buster Posey. "We've got our guy going tomorrow. Baseball is a funny game, you never know what will happen, but we feel good with him on the mound."

OCT 26, 2014 AT&T PARK

GIANTS 5 • ROYALS 0

BUMGARNER DOES IT AGAIN

SAN FRANCISCO, CALIFORNIA

Madison Bumgarner does not allow for unexpected results. Not this time of year.

Extending one of the greatest pitching streaks in postseason history, Bumgarner put San Francisco within one win of a third championship in five years Sunday night by leading the Giants to a 5-0 victory over the Kansas City Royals in Game 5 at AT&T Park.

For those wondering how it would be possible to improve on Bumgarner's Game 1 performance in Kansas City — three hits, one run in seven innings — there was nothing to it. He stepped on the Royals' necks

Facing Page: Starting pitcher Madison Bumgarner celebrates winning with catcher Buster Posey.
Icon Sportswire via AP Images

Above: Giants' Hunter Pence scores on an RBI double by Juan Perez as Kansas City Royals' Salvador Perez misses the ball.
AP Photo/Charlie Riedel

Kansas City Royals Salvador Perez watches as the Giants Brandon Crawford hits an RBI single.
AP Photo/Matt Slocum

from the very outset and never let them up for air, allowing four hits and no walks with eight strikeouts in a complete game.

The Royals advanced one runner past first base during Bumgarner's 117-pitch masterpiece, that coming on Omar Infante's double past diving leftfielder Travis Ishikawa in the fifth.

"I felt great all night," said the understated Bumgarner. "I'm not a big pitch-count guy. As long as you keep getting outs and you feel good, you should stay out there.

"This was a big game for us. It's a whole lot better going back to Kansas City to try to win one game instead of two."

The Royals hoped that Bumgarner would show up without his best stuff, with some cracks in his armor. But that's like hoping the waitress will give you the bill for the next table's

Giants' Juan Perez hits a two-run scoring double during the eighth inning of Game 5.
AP Photo/David J. Phillip

house salads instead of the three turf-and-surf entrées you ordered.

Could happen, but not likely.

"You could tell he was on early in the game," said Giants manager Bruce Bochy. "He didn't have any stressful innings. When he's on, he's fun to watch."

When the Giants scored three runs off the Royals' bullpen in the eighth inning to break open the game, Bochy could have removed

Above: Giants' Brandon Belt bunts for a single during the second inning of Game 5.
AP Photo/Charlie Riedel

Facing Page: Right fielder Hunter Pence and third baseman Pablo Sandoval celebrate scoring on a two-run double by left fielder Juan Perez (not shown) in the 8th inning.
Icon Sportswire via AP Images

Bumgarner and saved some bullets for possible Game 7 duty out of the pen but opted not to do so.

"Sure, I thought about taking him out," said Bochy, "but he was throwing the ball too good. The game wasn't over. I would have felt worse if I took him out and something would have happened."

Royals starter James Shields improved considerably from his Game 1 outing (five runs in three-plus innings), limiting the Giants to two runs over six innings. But good usually isn't good enough against Bumgarner, and that trend didn't change.

The Royals knew they'd be in trouble if Bumgarner was staked to an early lead and that's exactly what happened. The Giants took a 1-0 lead in the second inning, and the big play of that modest rally was Brandon Belt's bunt hit to the left side with

the Royals infield shifted to the right.

Such understated but smart plays make the Giants who they are — regular postseason participants. Their second run was a tribute to something else they do well — put the ball in play. With one on and two down in the fourth, Ishikawa hit a grounder past shortstop Alcides Escobar for a single and Brandon Crawford punched a knuckle curve from Shields into shallow left-center for an RBI hit.

The Giants have ridden the man they call "MadBum" hard to get within one victory of another World Series crown. Beginning with a wild-card shutout in Pittsburgh, he has pitched 472/3 innings over six starts while allowing only six earned runs (1.13 ERA).

"In the history of the game, there have been some great efforts, guys that have gone three games and things like that," said Bochy. "But I haven't seen a better pitcher over the course of this postseason. To do what he has done is pretty historic."

Facing Page: Madison Bumgarner salutes the San Francisco fans after his 5-0 shutout of the Royals. *Icon Sportswire via AP Images*

Giants 5, Royals 0
October 26, 2014, AT&T Park, San Francisco, CA

	1	2	3	4	5	6	7	8	9	R	H	E
KC	0	0	0	0	0	0	0	0	0	0	4	1
SF	0	1	0	1	0	0	0	3	–	5	12	0

ROYALS	AB	R	H	RBI	BB	SO	AVG
Escobar SS	4	0	0	0	0	0	.286
Gordon LF	4	0	0	0	0	1	.100
Cain RF-CF	4	0	1	0	0	0	.263
Hosmer 1B	4	0	1	0	0	1	.263
Perez C	3	0	1	0	0	0	.353
Moustakas 3B	3	0	0	0	0	1	.188
Infante 2B	3	0	1	0	0	1	.250
Herrera P	0	0	0	0	0	0	---
Davis P	0	0	0	0	0	0	---
Dyson CF	2	0	0	0	0	2	.222
Butler PH	1	0	0	0	0	1	.429
Aoki RF	0	0	0	0	0	0	.000
Shields P	2	0	0	0	0	1	.000
Nix 2B	1	0	0	0	0	0	.000
Totals	**31**	**0**	**4**	**0**	**0**	**8**	

2B – Infante (2, Bumgarner), **LOB** – 4

GIANTS	AB	R	H	RBI	BB	SO	AVG
Blanco CF	5	0	0	0	0	1	.200
Panik 2B	3	0	1	0	1	0	.250
Posey C	3	0	1	0	1	0	.211
Sandoval 3B	4	2	2	0	0	1	.364
Pence RF	4	2	2	0	0	1	.474
Belt 1B	4	0	1	0	0	2	.278
Ishikawa LF	3	0	2	0	0	0	.273
Perez PR-LF	1	1	1	2	0	0	.250
Crawford SS	4	0	2	3	0	0	.333
Bumgarner P	4	0	0	0	0	2	.000
Totals	**35**	**5**	**12**	**5**	**2**	**7**	

2B – Perez (1, Davis), **RBI** – Crawford 3 (3), Perez 2 (3), **LOB** – 8

ROYALS	IP	H	R	ER	BB	SO	ERA
Shields (L)	6.0	8	2	2	1	4	7.00
Herrera	1.0	2	2	2	1	0	4.50
Davis	1.0	2	1	0	0	3	0.00
Totals	**8.0**	**12**	**5**	**4**	**2**	**7**	

GIANTS	IP	H	R	ER	BB	SO	ERA
Bumgarner (W)	9.0	4	0	0	0	8	0.56
Totals	**9.0**	**4**	**0**	**0**	**0**	**8**	

Attendance – 43,087, **Game Time** – 3:09

ROYALS BATS COME ALIVE TO FORCE GAME 7

KANSAS CITY, MISSOURI

After San Francisco whipped Kansas City, 11-4, three days earlier to even things at two games apiece, Royals manager Ned Yost was asked if he had a feeling this World Series would go seven games.

"Oh, man, somewhere inside of me, secretly I had hoped that it would go seven games for the excitement and the thrill of it," Yost sincerely replied.

Yost doesn't have to wish for a Game 7 anymore. It will take place Wednesday night at Kauffman Stadium, and there's no telling how

Facing Page: San Franciscos' third baseman Pablo Sandoval expresses frustration at Kauffman Stadium. *Icon Sportswire via AP Images*

Above: Giants starting pitcher Jake Peavy leaves the game in the second inning after giving up five earned runs. *AP Photo/The Sacramento Bee,Jose Luis Villegas*

San Franciscos' Brandon Belt misses a tag on Kansas Citys' Alcides Escobar at first base during the second inning.
AP Photo/David J. Phillip

it might play out between these scrappy teams.

Thrilled to see somebody other than Madison Bumgarner on the mound Tuesday night for the Giants, the Royals erupted for seven runs in the second inning and cruised to a 10-0 victory in Game 6 to even the Series.

Kansas City had gone 16 innings without a run — including nine against Bumgarner in Game 5 — when Alex Gordon stepped to the plate in the bottom of the second

Royals' Omar Infante slides safely past Giants catcher Buster Posey during the fifth inning of Game 6. Infante scored from first on a double by Alcides Escobar.
AP Photo/Jeff Roberson

against Jake Peavy. When Gordon dunked a single into shallow center, there was no way to foresee the carnage that would follow.

Peavy would allow hits to five of the six hitters he faced before getting yanked. Norichika Aoki, who was 0 for 9 in the Series and benched in San Francisco, sent the veteran right-hander from the game with an RBI single that made it 2-0.

Hoping to stem the tide right there, Giants manager Bruce Bochy summoned reliever Yusmeiro Petit,

who had been impenetrable this postseason (12 scoreless innings). But Petit didn't have it this time and the seven-run outburst continued.

Lorenzo Cain singled in two runs. Eric Hosmer singled in two more after a Petit wild pitch.

Designated hitter Billy Butler, who had to sit under National League rules in San Francisco as the Royals' offense sputtered, doubled in the seventh run.

Peavy was charged with five runs and six hits in 1 1/3 innings, leaving

Royals Salvador Perez is safe at first as Giants Brandon Belt drops the ballduring the fourth inning.
AP Photo/Matt Slocum

with a career Series record of 0-2 with a 9.58 ERA in three starts.

"It's hugely disappointing. It's as disappointing as it can get," he said.

Kansas City's early explosion made it an easy night for rookie right-hander Yordano Ventura, who navigated through sporadic bouts of wildness to go seven shutout innings. He escaped his only trouble in the third, when he walked the bases loaded with one out and got Buster Posey to ground a 97 mph fastball into a double play.

"The best thing about this game is we get to wash it off," Bochy said. "It didn't go our way. The big inning killed us. But it's exciting for baseball, a seventh game with two teams going at it. It's do or die and that's how we'll approach it. We'll throw everything at them."

"I've never felt more strongly about us winning a ball game. I don't know why. It's just the confidence you see in these guys," said Yost. "That gives me confidence in them. I had a very, very strong feeling that whoever won Game 6 was going to win Game 7. We have to wait until tomorrow to see if my theory is correct."

Royals 10, Giants 0
October 28, 2014, Kauffman Stadium, Kansas City, MO

	1	2	3	4	5	6	7	8	9	R	H	E
SF	0	0	0	0	0	0	0	0	0	0	6	0
KC	0	7	1	0	1	0	1	0	–	10	15	0

GIANTS	AB	R	H	RBI	BB	SO	AVG
Blanco CF	4	0	0	0	1	2	.167
Panik 2B	3	0	1	0	1	0	.261
Posey C	3	0	0	0	0	0	.182
Susac C	1	0	0	0	0	0	.000
Sandoval 3B	3	0	1	0	1	0	.360
Arias 3B	0	0	0	0	0	0	.500
Pence RF	4	0	1	0	0	0	.435
Belt 1B	4	0	1	0	0	2	.273
Morse DH	4	0	0	0	0	0	.231
Ishikawa LF	2	0	0	0	1	2	.231
Perez LF	1	0	1	0	0	0	.333
Crawford SS	2	0	1	0	1	0	.350
Duffy SS	1	0	0	0	0	1	.500
Totals	**32**	**0**	**6**	**0**	**5**	**7**	

2B – Pence (3, Ventura), **LOB – 10**

ROYALS	AB	R	H	RBI	BB	SO	AVG
Escobar SS	5	1	2	1	0	0	.308
Aoki RF	3	1	1	1	1	1	.091
Dyson CF	1	0	0	0	0	0	.200
Cain CF-RF	3	1	2	3	2	0	.318
Hosmer 1B	5	1	2	2	0	2	.292
Butler DH	4	0	1	1	1	0	.364
Gordon LF	4	1	1	0	0	1	.125
Perez C	4	1	2	0	0	0	.381
Moustakas 3B	4	2	2	2	0	0	.250
Infante 2B	4	2	2	0	0	1	.300
Totals	**37**	**10**	**15**	**10**	**4**	**5**	

2B – Moustakas (2, Peavy); Hosmer (2, Petit); Butler (1, Petit); Infante (3, Machi); Cain (2, Machi); Escobar (3, Machi), **HR** – Moustakas (1, 7th inning off Strickland 0 on, 0 Out), **RBI** – Moustakas 2 (2), Aoki (1), Cain 3 (4), Hosmer 2 (4), Butler (3), Escobar (2), **LOB – 7**

GIANTS	IP	H	R	ER	BB	SO	ERA
Peavy (L)	1.1	6	5	5	1	2	12.79
Petit	0.2	3	2	2	0	0	4.91
Machi	3.0	5	2	2	1	2	8.10
Strickland	2.0	1	1	1	1	0	6.75
Vogelsong	1.0	0	0	0	1	1	9.82
Totals	**8.0**	**15**	**10**	**10**	**4**	**5**	

ROYALS	IP	H	R	ER	BB	SO	ERA
Ventura (W)	7.0	3	0	0	5	4	1.46
Frasor	1.0	2	0	0	0	1	3.86
Collins	1.0	1	0	0	0	2	3.60
Totals	**9.0**	**6**	**0**	**0**	**5**	**7**	

Attendance – 40,372, **Game Time** – 3:21

Starting pitcher Madison Bumgarner holds the MVP trophy after their 3-2 win against the Kansas City Royals.
AP Photo/Charlie Neibergall

OCT 29, 2014 KAUFFMAN STADIUM

GIANTS 3 • ROYALS 2

BUMGARNER LEADS GIANTS TO WORLD SERIES TITLE

KANSAS CITY, MISSOURI

There were many factors at play as the San Francisco Giants clinched their third World Series crown in five years Wednesday night by eliminating the Kansas City Royals with a nail-biting 3-2 victory in Game 7.

But, when you boiled it down, there was one primary difference that settled the issue: The Giants had Madison Bumgarner and the Royals didn't.

Bumgarner rescued the Giants for the third time in seven games, coming out of the bullpen to protect a one-run

Giants Madison Bumgarner, left, and catcher Buster Posey celebrate a win against the Kansas City Royals in Game 7 of baseball's World Series.
AP Photo/Charlie Riedel

San Franciscos' second baseman Joe Panik throws to San Francisco Giants shortstop Brandon Crawford for a double play getting Kansas City Royals center fielder Lorenzo Cain out.
AP Photo/The Sacramento Bee, Paul Kitagaki Jr.

lead with five innings of shutout ball at Kauffman Stadium.

Bumgarner allowed only two hits and was rewarded with a save to go with two victories and a sparkling 0.43 ERA. In 21 innings, he allowed nine hits and one run with only one walk and 17 strikeouts. Legendary stuff.

The Giants became the first team to win a World Series Game 7 on the road since the 1979 Pittsburgh Pirates. The last nine teams to play a Game 7 at home won the crown, but Bumgarner and Co. didn't worry about such trivia.

"Madison Bumgarner, what can you

say?" disappointed Royals manager Ned Yost said after the game. "They played great baseball. That's a special group of guys over there. They've got an outstanding manager, outstanding coaches and they play the game right."

The Giants always seem to play the game right when Bumgarner is on the mound

"I was just concentrating on making pitches," said Bumgarner, an easy choice as the World Series MVP. "I wasn't thinking about how many innings I'd go or how many pitches. We have one of the best closers in the game

Giants' Pablo Sandoval is safe at third on a ball hit by Brandon Belt as Kansas City Royals third baseman Mike Moustakas waits for the throw.
AP Photo/Charlie Riedel

(Santiago Casilla) out there. I'm glad my team believed in me and let me stay out there.

"I felt good still, relatively the same. This was as good as it gets, World Series Game 7. I was just thankful for the opportunity to get some big outs for the team. We're blessed to have the success we've had."

Both managers said before the game they would be quick with the hook if their starting pitchers stumbled, and they weren't kidding. When the Giants loaded the bases off Jeremy Guthrie

with no outs in the top of the second, Yost got rookie lefty Brandon Finnegan up in the pen.

Guthrie limited the damage to sacrifice flies by Michael Morse and Brandon Crawford, and the Royals went to work on Tim Hudson in the bottom of the inning. Billy Butler led off with a single and lumbered around to score on Alex Gordon's double to right-center.

When Hudson drilled Salvador Perez on the left thigh with a pitch, Giants manager Bruce Bochy got veteran

San Francisco' Michael Morse hits a
RBI-single off Kansas Citys' relief pitcher
Kelvin Herrera during the fourth inning.
AP Photo/Charlie Riedel

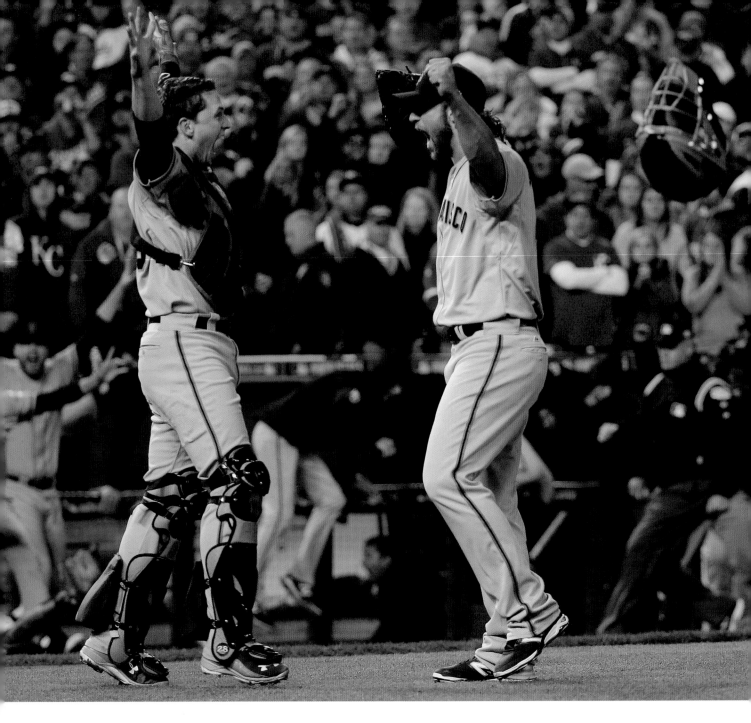

Giants' Madison Bumgarner, right, and catcher Buster Posey celebrate a win of baseball's 2014 World Series.
AP Photo/David J. Phillip

lefty Jeremy Affeldt up in the bullpen. A sacrifice fly by Omar Infante tied the score later in the inning and when Alcides Escobar followed with a single, Bochy replaced Hudson with Affeldt.

It was a miserable World Series for any Giants starter not named Madison Bumgarner. In five appearances, the other three starters went a mere 161/3 innings, allowing 18 runs for a 9.92 ERA.

Giants DH Michael Morse made it

a 3-2 game in the fourth with an RBI single off hard-throwing reliever Kelvin Herrera, who took over for Guthrie with runners on the corners and one down. It was a great piece of hitting by Morse, who was jammed by a 0-2 fastball at 99 mph that broke his bat, but he fought it off into right field.

Affeldt got the visitors to the fifth inning with that one-run lead, and Bochy waited no longer to summon Bumgarner. He worked around a leadoff hit by Infante for a scoreless frame, but he wasn't done.

After Infante's single, Bumgarner retired the next 14 hitters before encountering his only tense moment. With two down in the ninth, Gordon sent a sinking drive to left-center that Gregor Blanco let get by and roll to the wall. The Giants had trouble getting the ball back in, allowing Gordon to race to third base.

Undaunted, Bumgarner retired Perez on a foul pop to Sandoval to silence the crowd and trigger a mob scene of Giants piling on top of each other on the infield grass.

"I figured this would be a close game," said Bochy, who became the 10th manager to win three World Series titles. "I still had trust in this guy. No way I'd take him out unless he asked. He's really amazing. We just stayed on that horse and rode it."

Giants 3, Royals 2
October 29, 2014, Kauffman Stadium, Kansas City, MO

	1	2	3	4	5	6	7	8	9	R	H	E
SF	0	2	0	1	0	0	0	0	0	3	8	1
KC	0	2	0	0	0	0	0	0	0	2	6	0

GIANTS	AB	R	H	RBI	BB	SO	AVG
Blanco CF	4	0	0	0	0	0	.143
Panik 2B	4	0	0	0	0	3	.222
Posey C	4	0	0	0	0	2	.154
Sandoval 3B	3	2	3	0	0	0	.429
Pence RF	4	1	2	0	0	0	.444
Belt 1B	4	0	2	0	0	0	.308
Morse DH	3	0	1	2	0	2	.250
Crawford SS	3	0	0	1	0	3	.304
Perez LF	3	0	0	0	0	2	.250
Totals	**32**	**3**	**8**	**3**	**0**	**12**	

2B – Sandoval (3, Davis), **RBI** – Morse 2 (4), Crawford (4), **SF** – Morse, Crawford, **LOB** – 5

ROYALS	AB	R	H	RBI	BB	SO	AVG
Escobar SS	3	0	1	0	0	1	.310
Aoki RF	3	0	0	0	1	0	.071
Cain CF	4	0	1	0	0	1	.308
Hosmer 1B	4	0	0	0	0	2	.250
Butler DH	4	1	1	0	0	0	.333
Gordon LF	3	1	2	1	0	0	.185
Perez C	3	0	0	0	0	0	.333
Moustakas 3B	3	0	0	0	0	0	.217
Infante 2B	2	0	1	1	0	1	.318
Totals	**29**	**2**	**6**	**2**	**1**	**5**	

2B – Gordon (3, Hudson), **RBI** – Gordon (2), Infante (5), **S** – Escobar, **SF** – Infante, **LOB** – 5

GIANTS	IP	H	R	ER	BB	SO	ERA
Hudson	1.2	3	2	2	1	1	6.14
Affeldt	2.1	1	0	0	0	0	0.00
Bumgarner (W)	5.0	2	0	0	0	4	0.43
Totals	**9.0**	**6**	**2**	**2**	**1**	**5**	

ROYALS	IP	H	R	ER	BB	SO	ERA
Guthrie (L)	3.1	4	3	3	0	3	5.40
Herrera	2.2	3	0	0	0	4	2.70
Davis	2.0	1	0	0	0	3	0.00
Holland	1.0	0	0	0	0	2	0.00
Totals	**9.0**	**8**	**3**	**3**	**0**	**12**	

Attendance – 40,535, **Game Time** – 3:10

San Francisco Giants players in the dugout celebrate after game 7 of the 2014 World Series.
AP Photo/Matt Slocum